Foreword by Carrie Gilmer

Love,

O W P

A Compilation of Many of my
2010 &2011 Facebook Statuses

PROPHETESS O.W. PETCOFF

Love, OWP

Copyright © 2012
Onoma Ministries and Publications
First Printing 2012
ISBN: 0-9701184-6-5/978-0-9701184-6-2

Facebook is a trademark of Facebook, Inc.

Scripture quotations are taken from the
Holy Bible, King James Version
Copyright © 1996, Thomas Nelson, Inc.

Published by:
Onoma Ministries and Publications,
Arlington, TX
prophetessowp@aol.com

Table of Contents

Foreword

About the Author

Foreword

I have never met Omonpee Petcoff in person; I hope with all hope some day that I shall. We have a mutual friend on Facebook and after enjoying each other's comments, we said to each other, "Hey, why don't we become friends?" Since then we have made each other laugh, and think. We have supported, reminded, encouraged and come alongside each other. We've helped each other stand. That's what friendship is. Omonpee Petcoff is my friend, even though I've never met her in person.

O monpee says she is a Prophetess. At first, I was not used to using that term in this way. Where I come from people think of a Prophet as a rare (in chronological time) sort of fortune teller or predictor of the future. "The world is gonna end on May 12, 2012." But that is not the kind of "fortune" or "future" Prophets predict. They have a gift of discerning right from wrong. As all behavior has consequences, they have a gift of wisdom in predicting consequences and speaking up. On the roads in life, Prophets are the warning, or caution, or STOP signs.

W e all have the capability of knowing right from wrong, good from evil, or we should have. Wisdom is the understanding of what to do with that knowledge. Sometimes, for lots of reasons, it is hard to see even what is right or wrong. The road ahead is covered in dense fog, or maybe it is under construction. We need some road signs telling us about the possible terrain or traffic or potholes ahead.

It's been this way, according to the biblical account, right from the beginning. Adam and Eve were together in the Garden when she began to be tempted by the fruit that she had been warned would crush her life. She began to rationalize it would be okay. Maybe it was even good. Her knowledge of good and evil however, was covered in dense fog. She did not have it. And what did Adam do? Did he warn? Did he yell stop? Did he remind her of what they had been told? No! He stood there and waited to see what would happen. And when she did not die immediately, he ate some too. So they fell together; rather than stand together. When Eve "saw" that IT was "good", Adam was uncertain but he did not say anything. He did not speak up. Omonpee is not uncertain. Omonpee has no problem speaking up!

According to the account, Adam and Eve did not have the knowledge of right and wrong yet. But they had the knowledge of what they had been told. When my oldest son was about 4 and 5 he used to run into the street, without looking! He would see something on the other side, it would grab his attention, and he would run toward it. Maybe it was a friend, maybe a squirrel, maybe the garbage man or postal worker. I mean it was happening almost everyday I let him outside. I watched him but I could not be there every second! I was worried he was going to be hit by a car. Of course at first I said, "You can't run into the street! You have to look! You could get hit by a car and killed!" But he was 4 or 5. I realized "killed" and "die" had no meaning to him; the warning was not clear to him. I needed to make it clear and understandable!

I found a pop can that had been run over and flattened. I found another that was as it should be. I showed it to him and said, "You see this?", holding up the flattened can, "This is what will happen to you if you keep running into the street without looking!"

P rophets tell it like it is. They clear the fog. They have a gift at removing the rationalizations. They see if it is or is not "good" and they speak up! This is what Omonpee does. Keep doing that, that way, and it will crush your growth as a Christian, it will crush your marriage, your finances, your job, your relationships, your health, etcetera, etcetera.

O monpee is like the robot on the old television series "Lost In Space". "Warning! Warning! Danger! Danger!" Are you lost in space? Listen up people.

Carrie Gilmer,
Facebook-friend-turned-real-life-friend-of-Omonpee

Preface

Dearest Readers,

I would like to take this opportunity to present the book that wrote itself...and that was almost never written!

In 2009, my brother-in-law was in the Air Force and being deployed to Afghanistan. He suggested that all the family members keep in contact through Facebook. I, who had shunned all manner of social networking up until that time, was very reluctant at first. Coincidentally, at the same time, my sister was telling me about Facebook and urging me to join. With "encouragement" from both sides of the family, I decided to bite the bullet and signed up for an account. "But, " I said to myself, "this is with the understanding that I use this page sparingly, if at all." Not being much of a socializer (as is usually the case with people who are called to prophetic ministry), I purposed to keep to myself and not be "chatting" or whatever people did on these things (didn't know) all the time.

Well, that didn't last.

I don't quite know when and how it happened, but, one contact led to another; one high school classmate added me and another sent a friend request, and so on and so on. "Okay," I thought, "these are people from back home. I guess it would be okay to add them. But no more." But, not only did I add classmates. I ended up adding more family members. Then, I found people with similar interests as mind – Christianity, autism intervention, thyroid cancer (later) – and forged virtual relationships with these people; people who, except for their profile pic, I had never laid eyes on in life!

And, then, the posting began.

Being a minister and a Christian writer (a Journalism major and English minor in college, too), I love to write about things of the Lord! So, then, to have this venue in which I can post *real time* messages – "What's on your mind?" – and relay them *at that moment* and get feedback from people was a Godsend! And, as I began to post these revelations that God was giving me, I noticed that more and more people added me! They were interested in what God was saying through me; it was ministering to them! And, in time, they began to trust the God in me! It was phenomenal to me!

And, I kept posting…and posting…and posting.

In 2010, I was diagnosed with thyroid cancer. Again, through Facebook, I was able to find people who were also diagnosed with thyroid cancer, many of whom are some of my real-life friends to this day! We helped each other through some hard times, including diagnosis, treatment and the aftermath of life without a thyroid. One symptom of not having the thyroid hormones regulated is irregular sleep patterns. I would find myself up posting all times of the day and night. But, there was always someone there to talk with me, listen to me, pray for me, as I now had friends from all over the world!

And, I kept posting…and posting….and posting.

I would post about my day. I would post about my son Desmond who has been diagnosed with Pervasive Developmental Disorder, Not Otherwise

Specified (PDD-NOS), a form of autism; he has risen above many challenges and has become a successful student and a hardworking young man. I would post about my husband Ron (who now has his own Facebook wall, too), a hardworking and loving man. When I could not sleep at night, I would post about my challenges with late night food cravings. When the silly moods would hit me, I would post about all garden-variety foolishness (within reason, though ☺). Speaking of silliness, I would post about my dear elderly friend Mrs. Harper, who is funny and needs her own sitcom. Mostly and primarily, though, I would post the revelations of the Word of God that the Lord gave me.

My nature is to post in a conversational manner, taking complex revelations and presenting them in a manner that all can understand. I am also directed by God to use many of my own life experiences as teaching tools, making parables out of them. I am, indeed, a living epistle, known and read of men.

Pretty soon, I had many, many posts! And, I had many, many Facebook friends!

Again, being a writer and a publisher, I have books "on the brain" ☺. That is the way God made me. So, then, when I began to see these statuses amass…and that the people who read them commented that they were blessed by them on a daily basis…I felt the Lord leading me to compile a book of these statuses.

This book – *Love, OWP* – is a compilation of most of my Facebook statuses from 2010 and 2011. The title comes from the way I commonly close out many correspondences on Facebook and when I am ministering via email/inbox. Compiling the book was a labor of love (a lot of mouse work, cutting and pasting from Facebook into the book file). And, while I did not leave out very many of my statuses, I did leave out some. The Holy Spirit did not lead me to include some and some I left out because people who are not my Facebook friends and who have not developed a "relationship" with me would not "get " them (the sillier ones and the ones where I am using alliteration [usually these are silly]). For instance, all but one of the posts about Mrs. Harper was omitted☺.

Key to Understanding

As you read this book, if you are not used to my Facebook posts, you may need a key to understanding my writing. Here is a basic key:

- **FBFs** – Short for Facebook friends. I use this a lot.
- *SCREAMING ROFL* – Literally, me SCREAMING with laughter ☺
- *HOWLING ROFL* – Exuberant laughter on my part ☺
- ☺, :-), ☹, :-D – I smile a lot when I am typing and want to convey that in my statuses.
- *CAPITAL LETTERS* – Facebook to date does not have a **bold** function or an *italic* function in statuses. I am not shouting by using all caps; it is strictly for emphasis.
- *LOVE YOU/♥ YOU!/HEARTS IN GENERAL* – I truly love my Facebook friends and want them to tell them every chance I get.
- **THEMES OF MY MINISTRY** – Again, my FBFs know this, but, my ministry focuses on many themes including the prophetic, dealing with rejection, correcting Christian leadership. But, I also have passions for autism intervention, education and thyroid cancer awareness. All of these facets are covered in my statuses.

- **MY NAMES** – Omonpee, Pay, OWP, O.W. Petcoff, Prophetess Petcoff (I have a status about this). I usually refer to myself as Omonpee. Other people refer to me as they have relationship with me.
- **"OMONPEE is…"** – On FB, your profile picture is positioned so that you can use it to replace your name or "I." When I copied and pasted these, the sentences started with "is…". In many instances in the book, I typed in Omonpee.

Polka Dotted Presents

This book is my way of saying, "Thank you" to my dear, dear Facebook friends, for all of their support and love. They have been through some trying times with me – cancer, the death of my brother, ill health in general, problems with the education system as relates to my son – and have remained faithful, reading my posts everyday and supporting my ministry. (Speaking of "Thank you", let me stop right here and say *thanks to Carrie Gilmer* – my Facebook-friend-turned-real-life-friend – *for writing the Foreword to this book*. Carrie, I ♥ you and appreciate you so much!) I hope that by my putting these posts in one compact source, all of my Facebook friends who care to do so can use this little book as a source of encouragement, laughter, strength and can be ministered to again and again by the posts.

Some may ask, "Why the polka dots / present (gift) theme on the cover? What does that have to do with Facebook?" Again, my FBFs will remember that I have a "thing" with alliteration (stringing words that begin with the same letter, to convey a message). Most of my alliteration is of words with the letter P (works out well, as my last name – Petcoff – begins with P). *This book is my GIFT* – hence the giftwrap and bow – to you, my Facebook friends and to others who wish to read it. My

FBFs also know that I go through certain "phases" of affinity to certain things (clothing and eyewear, for example) and share pics of these things on Facebook. Right now, the Lord has me in a polka dot phase – clothing, accessories, etc. - with the polka dots being in the pattern on the cover. So, then, in sharing the polka dots, I am, again, sharing part of my personal story, presenting it as a gift to my dear Facebook friends.

That being said, following is some of my "trademark" alliteration, with a special message just for my Facebook friends and "new" readers:

"Prophetess Pay Petcoff is positively proud to present this polka-dotted packaged present to precious people – preachers, prophets, parishioners, prized-pals!

Please peruse the pages of this pint-sized paperback publication and partake of the plentiful passages and posts of passionate and purposeful public pontificating."

Love.

2010

STATUSES

 PHIL. 3:13

O.W. PETCOFF'S PERSONAL INTERPRETATION
(FOR HERSELF) OF PHILLIPPIANS 3:13 –

"I may not have it all figured out. But, if I don't know anything else, I know this: I cannot go forward while looking backward. In 2011, anything LEFT BEHIND STAYS BEHIND! I'm purposing to not even let it cross my mind. I'm moving on to NEWER, BIGGER AND BETTER."

 KEEP YOUR COOL

"In all this, Job sinned not, nor charged God foolishly."
- Job 1:22 KJV

REVELATION: No matter what you are going through, have gone through, or will go through, KEEP YOUR COOL. Remember WHO YOU ARE, WHAT YOU STAND FOR AND WHAT YOU WILL AND WILL NOT TOLERATE/ALLOW. Don't lower your standards or expectations - of OTHERS or YOURSELF - in times of trouble. It will soon pass!

 WHAT IT LOOKS LIKE

When you are CALLED, your PAIN-BIRTHED RESILIENCE looks like "STRENGTH" to people. When you are CALLED, your SACRIFICE-BORN ANOINTING looks like "LUCK" to people. When you are CALLED, your TRIBULATION-PERFECTED ASSUREDNESS looks like "ARROGANCE" to people. Looks, can indeed, be deceiving.

1

Love, OWP

LANGUAGE BARRIER

At the Tower of Babel, God Himself brought DIVISION among the people by causing them to speak DIFFERENT LANGUAGES and different dialects within those languages. He did so that they would SEPARATE into groups of like-language people and not complete the tower.

REVELATION: Sometimes GOD HIMSELF will cause you and people you know to begin to SPEAK DIFFERENT LANGUAGES so that you are not COMMUNICATING like you once did. Even if He has to ALLOW the enemy to wreak havoc in the relationship, it is HIS PLAN that the relationship dissolves and you all part ways. He does this so that you will BE FORCED to LET GO, MOVE ON. Sometimes, if they are not SPEAKING YOUR LANGUAGE ANYMORE or YOU ARE NOT SPEAKING THEIRS, it's time to move on!

COCKROACHES

COCKROACHES CONGREGATE IN THE DARK. BUT, WHEN YOU TURN ON A LIGHT, THEY SCATTER. THEY GET ALL DISCOMBOBULATED AND AGITATED. WHEN GOD SENDS YOU - A LIGHT - INTO DARK, EVIL PLACES, MARVEL NOT WHEN YOU ARE NOT RECEIVED BY PEOPLE WITH A ROACH SPIRIT, WHO RUN WHEN THEY SEE YOU COMING AND ACT LIKE THEY HATE YOU JUST FOR BREATHING; THEY ARE UNCOMFORTABLE....

 ## ASSEMBLY

I understand more and more WHY the Bible says that EVERY ONE of us has to work out OUR OWN salvation. Religion has taught us to "CONGREGATE", while the Bible says ASSEMBLE YOURSELVES. An ASSEMBLY is the culmination of DISTINCT, INDIVIDUAL PARTS coming together to create a WHOLE. We must know OUR PART and remain true to that. Our PART is that for which God holds us responsible.

 ## UNDERSTANDING

♫A-B-C-D-E-F-G/H-I-J-K-ELLEM and OPY♫ -

REVELATION: Even after HEARING the Word/Prophecy/Scripture/Revelation - NO MATTER HOW SIMPLE/EASY TO UNDERSTAND IT MAY SEEM - make sure you have CLARITY. "In all that getting, get an understanding." "Study to show thyself APPROVED, a workman that NEEDETH NOT BE ASHAMED, RIGHTLY DIVIDING the WORD OF TRUTH."

 ## "I WAS WRONG!"

When you can admit that you are wrong and/or you made a mistake, you take the ammunition away those who would use your mistakes against you.

❦ READY FOR BUSINESS ❦

Then ninety-year-old Missionary Genieve Denson
would tell me the story of her being denied an ASPIRIN
while she was in the hospital. They told her they were
out. As only she could tell it, she replied, "Umph! All
this big ol' hospital and NO ASPIRIN!" :-)

REVELATION: I had contemplated shutting down my
FB account because of something I experienced recently.
But, even today, God showed me that people actually
STOP BY my wall to READ what God gives me; they
STOP BY LOOKING FOR SOMETHING. Those people
are looking and have grown accustom to being able to
come by and hear what God is saying through me on
this lil ol' wall :-).
As Christians (particularly, but not limited to, those of
us who are ministers), we have to remember that we are
not saved merely for ourselves, but to be a beacon for
someone else. That being said, unlike Mrs. Denson's
HOSPITAL and the aspirin incident, we have to remain
"stocked up" with the Word, being able to help those
that God would send our way. Mrs. Denson was in the
hospital for "serious" illness; had the hospital been
closed, she would have died. We, likewise, must make
ourselves AVAILABLE for the Master's Use and in the
Service of God by serving others and providing comfort
(SPIRITUAL ASPIRIN) to those in need.

So, I am open for business and fully stocked up on
spiritual aspirin.

BLESSINGS IN STORE

I am seeing "Martin" on television and remembering that, on that show, it was NEVER revealed what Tommy did for a living! Martin's famous line, "Tommy ain't got no job!", became a famous punch line :-). Tommy's job (or, perhaps, the lack thereof) became one of the best-kept secrets in television history.

REVELATION - SOMETIMES, GOD HAS YOU HIDDEN, RIGHT OUT IN THE OPEN! God has to HIDE US from others who would hinder your PURPOSE AND DESTINY; Sometimes God has to HIDE US FROM OURSELVES until we are ready to handle WHO WE REALLY ARE and WHAT... GOD HAS IN STORE FOR US!

People who are quick to say, "She ain't got no husband!" or "He ain't got no future!", "They ain't got no chance." just don't know! They don't know what God has FOR you and IN you.

"EYES HAVE NOT SEEN, NEITHER HAVE EARS HEARD, NEITHER HATH IT ENTERED INTO THE HEARTS OF MEN THE THINGS THAT GOD HATH PREPARED FOR THEM THAT LOVE HIM."

AFFIRMATION

REVELATION - The NEED for AFFIRMATION can lead to RUINATION!

RIGHTFUL HEIRS

When my son was younger (like last year), he would come in from school, go to the refrigerator and ASK for things he saw (like sodas, snacks, etc.). As he MATURED (this year), he still comes in and goes straight to the 'fridge, but he no longer ASKS. He knows what is in there he is welcome to; he knows his RIGHTS AS A SON/HEIR.

He is COMFORTABLE enough in his RIGHTS as well as his relationship to THE FATHER (and the mother) so that he no longer asks for everything (and my root beer now comes up missing :-)).

We, too, need to be COMFORTABLE in our RELATIONSHIP to God, the Father and know our RIGHTS as HEIRS/JOINT HEIRS WITH CHRIST. Some stuff we need to pray about and some we just need to "go get."

ENLARGED TERRITORY

People are quick to quote The Prayer of Jabez, particularly the part about, "Enlarge my territory." I have heard preachers equating this with getting more money, cars, notoriety, etc. But, when our TERRITORY is enlarged, SO IS OUR REALM OF RESPONSIBILITY. To whom much is given, much is required! Territory is not "enlarged" for us to just "look cute" or "be important." Territory is enlarged for ASSIGNMENT.

RESISTANCE IS FUTILE

(WARNING :-))STAR TREK:THE NEXT GENERATION REFERENCE FOLLOWS- The religious system is like the BORG, always trying to get someone to ASSIMILATE. When a person joins a church that subscribes to BORG mentality, ALL EXPRESSIONS OF INDIVIDUALITY ARE PUNISHED AND DISCOURAGED. They put God in a "BOX." If you want to fit in, you must CONFORM to the doctrine. If you want to fit in, RESISTANCE IS FUTILE.

SEASONS CHANGE

My best friend is a honey connoisseur; she loves all types. She said that this year one of the honeys tastes different; the store told her it was because the pollen was different because THE SEASON HAD CHANGED. My friend said that she wishes she would have stocked up last season.

REVELATION: Seasons change. Get/do all that you are supposed to get/do in the CURRENT season, because once it's gone, it's gone. Don't miss your opportunity! Don't miss your blessing! TRUE MINISTRY is that which reaches the INDIVIDUAL first and then expands to the masses. "Despise the not day of small beginnings," "If you are faithful over a few things, I'll make you ruler over many," "leaving the flock behind to go find the ONE lost sheep (paraphrasing)", etc. God is not concerned about MEGAMINISTRIES, BIG OFFERINGS, TITLES AND POSITIONS. If you DO THE WORK and minister to the ONE, then to the FEW, He will be able to trust you not to lose your mind and do the fool with the MANY.

Love, OWP

HARMONY IN THE BODY

Choirs sing in harmony, with each member or group singing its part (bass, tenor, contralto, alto, soprano, mezzo soprano) according to the God-given range of each person's voice. When these voices blend, they make ONE COMPLETE SOUND; THEY ARE IN HARMONY. Yet, within the Body of Christ, we want everybody to SOUND JUST LIKE US and do not EMBRACE the God-given DIFFERENCES.

"But now [are they] many members, yet but one body.

And the eye cannot say unto the hand, I have no need of thee: nor again the head to the feet, I have no need of you.

Nay, much more those members of the body, which seem to be more feeble, are necessary:

And those [members] of the body, which we think to be less honourable, upon these we bestow more abundant honour; and our uncomely [parts] have more abundant comeliness."
- I Corinthians 12:20-23 KJV

We miss the point that, when joined together, WE ARE SUPPOSED TO MAKE ONE BODY and not be just a bunch of EYES, or NOSES or EARS, ETC. It is the sum of our individual parts that will bring us VICTORY as a Body. HARMONY IS A MUST!

Different people have different ministries. And, the focuses of their ministries may be different. I have FBFs from varied walks of life with various ministries. And, even among the ones who have the same CALLINGS, the focuses of their ministries are different. For instance, I have several FBFs who are prophets. Yet within that group, I have a prophetess friend whose mantle is to WARN the people of destruction that comes when we are disobedient. Then I have a prophet FBF whose mantle is more of a TEACHING mantle. The "JOB TITLES" are the same, but the "DESCRIPTIONS" are different. But, ONE IS NOT ANY MORE OF A "TRUE PROPHET" THAN THE OTHER ONE and both are important in God's Eyes.

I am reminded of the book, "Animal Farm" by George Orwell. In this book, the farm animals had been mistreated by the farmer for years. They joined forces to overthrow him. However, the pigs began to act just like the farmer! That's how it is with some in the church. We come out of darkness and out of bad situations. Then, we get a calling and, if we are not careful we tend to look down on others, just as we were looked down on once upon a time. We are all in this together, especially if we are a BODY.

EATING RIGHT

We cannot blame all of our woes on Satan. Some things we bring on ourselves. If you are OBESE or have a diagnosis of HIGH BLOOD PRESSURE, and you eat EVERYTHING IN SIGHT, most of which is full of salt, fat and sugars, YOU NEEDN'T cast out "a spirit of obesity; a spirit of diabetes." Now, you can maybe cast a spirit of GLUTTONY out of you, but, PUSH AWAY FROM THE TABLE. Help YOURSELF!

Love. OWP

❦ OVERWATERING ❦

When I was growing up, my mom sometimes had houseplants. Once, I wanted to water one of them. She supervised me to make sure that did not OVER WATER the plant. I could not understand HOW you could over water a plant; I thought water was good for plants. But, you can essentially DROWN the poor plant with too much water.

In reference to winning souls to Christ and teaching spiritual matters, the Bible says that, "Some plant, some water, but God gives the increase." Water represents the WORD OF GOD. We as Christians MUST BE CAREFUL NOT TO OVER WATER when we are ministering. It can KILL and/or SEVERELY STUNT THE GROWTH of the poor little seed that has just been planted!

REVELATION: Leave people alone! Once you have planted the seed and/or spoken the Word that God has given you for them, do not continue to SPEAK HARSH WORDS of condemnation, etc. The same God that saved YOU and delivered YOU will deal with that person.

❦ WHO'S WEIRD? ❦

John the Baptist - walked around the desert unkempt and wooly, preaching to anyone who would listen, eating locusts and honey; Isaiah - preached NAKED; Noah - built an Ark before rain was ever heard of; All of these Biblical figures were considered WEIRD; FRINGE PEOPLE. And, yet, God CHOSE to USE THEM mightily. REVELATION: Be careful of who you shun and discount; they just may be God's Anointed.

CONFUSION CEASES

I was trying to watch my much-anticipated episode of "The Next Iron Chef" that I missed earlier tonight, when I heard the following in my spirit and was led to share it:

"Things that were confusing for years will now become crystal clear. All of it will come together to create a crystal clear picture of where you have been, where you are and where you are going. Indeed, you will SEE the manifestation of ALL THINGS WORKING TOGETHER for your GOOD but also for the YOUR PURPOSE to be manifested. It now all makes sense!"

SECULAR MINISTRY

The term "secular ministry" is an oxymoron and maybe even a misnomer. People use the term to denote people whose callings are in the workplace, etc., and NOT behind the pulpit or in a church. But, ALL ministry is ministry. And, ALL ministry should be, at least in part, SECULAR, so to speak. "GO YE INTO THE HIGHWAYS AND HEDGES..."Ministry that is confined to the four walls of the church building is not effective ministry.

MATURITY

Butterflies do not re-enter cocoons...or not without a lot of discomfort. He that hath ears...

Love, OWP

🎀 LANGUAGE BARRIER 🎀

Don't be envious of a person who has stepped into his or her season. What looks like an overnight success is, more than likely, the MANIFESTATION of a SEED that was PLANTED in the SPIRIT via VISION, GERMINATED in the SOUL, WATERED with MANY TEARS and NURTURED with CONSISTENT HARD WORK, SACRIFICE and DETERMINATION.

🎀 ISOLATION 🎀

I turned late to "Iron Chef America" on Food Network. The chefs - Iron and challenger - normally have sous chefs to help them. Don't know why, but the challenger was going it alone and looking very comfortable; I get the feeling that maybe his sous chefs could not make it. But, he did not let that stop him.

REVELATION: SOMETIMES God will let you go through long periods of ISOLATION and DOING THINGS WITH NO HELP to PREPARE you to do things on your own EVEN WHEN HE SENDS PEOPLE WHO ARE TO HELP YOU BUT THEY FLAKE OUT ON YOU. Having "people" does not always mean that they will be available, willing or able to help you when you need it. But, the person who has spent time alone - alone with God and with himself or herself - develops needed skills to MAKE IT, with or without anyone else around.

12

 # BREAD, PLEASE

The Bible says, "Man does not live by bread alone, but by every word that proceedeth out of the mouth of God." (Matt. 4:4) Christians quote this with no importance on the word ALONE. While "every word" of the Lord is IMPORTANT and reigns supreme, this scripture does NOT say that we DO NOT NEED "bread."

Even Jesus provided PHYSICAL FOOD for the hungry crowd while He ministered SPIRITUAL FOOD to them (Mark 6:41). Let us not be so SPIRITUALLY MINDED until we are NO EARTHLY GOOD.

 # ANOINTING

Michael Jackson did not invent the Moonwalk, but he DID make it famous. His anointing and gifting caused it to catch on and became associated almost synonymously with MJ; it became one of his signature moves and made him even more famous than he had been in his earlier career. Col. Sanders did not invent the chicken. Disney did not write "Winnie the Pooh", "Sleeping Beauty", nor "Cinderella".

REVELATION: While God will give us CREATIONS and INVENTIONS, we do not always have to "reinvent the wheel (or The Moonwalk, or whatever)." Sometimes, all we have to do is DISCERN what HE has allowed to cross our path, lay hold of it, and infuse it with our spiritual DNA - our "divinely nurtured anointing." It is the ANOINTING that makes the difference.

Love, OWP

 ## PRAYER

A LITTLE DITTY ABOUT PRAYER:

When asked to pray for someone,
we don't need to know, "WHY?",
If you are really going to pray,
then you don't have to PRY.
If you are going to pray, then, pray,
but if not, then JUST DON'T.
But, if asked to pray don't say, "I will",
When you know good and well that you WON'T.
- OWP

 ## TIED DOWN

In Matthew 21:1-3, Jesus directs the disciples to go find a donkey and a colt that have been tied up. He tells them to tell anyone who asks that HE had need of the donkey and the colt.

REVELATION: Sometimes when we feel tied down and like we are not going anywhere in our lives, God has KEPT and PRESERVED us to be used by HIM for a specific time and season. Sometimes, in our waiting, we are tied to DIVINE PURPOSE.

 ## THE WORLD CUP

Jesus CONQUERED the "WORLD CUP" at Gethesamane: "And he went a little farther, and fell on his face, and prayed, saying, O my Father, if it be possible, let this CUP pass from me: neverthless, not as I will, but as thou wilt." - Matthew 26:39 KJV

14

 ## DETOX TIP #1

Omonpee's DETOX AND STRESS MANAGEMENT TIP #1: Don't ask questions that will have answers you are not prepared to handle without getting stressed out. Whatever it is has already happened and, if there is nothing you can do to change it, why ask a question, only to get an answer that is going to get you worked up? Wait until it no longer presses that button and then discuss it.

 ## DETOX TIP #2

Omonpee's DETOX AND STRESS MANAGEMENT TIP #2 - While detoxing - physically, spiritually, emotionally - you are going to feel worse before you are detoxed completely. You will have really high highs, but you will also have really low lows. This is because the toxin/"toxin" is working its way up and out. Do not get discouraged and stop the process because of the lows.

"Let patience have its perfect work, that you may be perfect and entire wanting nothing."

 ## DETOX TIP #3

Omonpee's DETOX AND STRESS MANAGEMENT TIP #3 - When you are getting rid of toxins/"toxins", you must ~~IGNORE HIDE DELETE~~ BLOCK irritants from your life. Ignoring, hiding and deleting keeps the door open for future contamination. (Just got that a few seconds ago ☺)

15

Love, OWP

 ## HONESTY

If I smelled bad, would y'all ♥ me enough to tell me that I STINK? I mean, if I was sho' 'nuff cuttin' up, rank and foul, would any of you care enough about me to not allow me to go around smelling like that?

I hope you would, and I would most certainly appreciate it. And, some would. Yet, SIN is a stench in God's Nostrils, but we, His Representatives (ministers, this is for you) do not address people's sins. WE LET THEM GO AROUND STINKING LITERALLY TO HIGH HEAVEN. Do we love them/Him more than we fear people getting angry when we tell them?

 ## *"JUST PRAY ABOUT IT"*

Omonpee is thinking about the areas of her life that have caused her the most pain and the times that she sought counsel concerning them. Well-meaning ministers sometimes make light of others' needs because they do not struggle in those areas themselves. "Just pray about it" does not always help. If it did, they would not need counsel. Even Jesus left a blueprint for prayer because we do not always know what to pray.

 ## THE DESPISED ONES

Some people are called to lead controversial lives. They are called to be hated, rejected, persecuted, misunderstood, alienated, talked about, lied on and spat on. This life style is not for everyone, but it is the portion of those who are called to this. In many ways, this was Jesus' lot in life. Do we REALLY want to be like Him?

REAL TREASURE

Recent post about moths eating holes in my St. John skirt reminded me of: "But lay up for yourself treasures in heaven, where neither moth nor dust doth corrupt..." - Matt. 6:20a-b KJV.

We have to be careful what we treasure; our priorities must be KINGDOM ORIENTED. We can have nice things, but we do not LIVE for them; they are mere THINGS. Only what we do for Christ will last.

I love St. John, but I have changed kids' poopy diapers while wearing it :-). I also minister in it; it is my "work clothing". I have also given more of it away than most people will ever own in their lives, and a lot of it I don't even remember. It is merely a tool with which I did/do what God commanded me. I love it,
but I love God more!

When we get to the point that EVERYTHING we have - no matter how expensive, how rare, how cherished - belongs to God and is mete for His Use in the Kingdom, He can bless us with more because we will not worship the stuff, but will allow it to be used for God's Glory

The Bible says that the streets of Heaven are paved with gold. How little does God care about the MONETARY value of material things that He would pave the STREETS with gold! He only cares that it was what He wanted to use to accomplish the building of the streets; it was a means to an end, but not the end. Oftimes, we get the "stuff" and that is the END-ALL for a lot of people. God is not pleased with that mentality.

17

Love. OWP

 # KNOWING

One strategy of the enemy is to try to make you doubt yourself – doubt who you are, what God has spoken to you, your ability to do what you know you can because you've done it before and/or because God told you you could. He is a liar! God knows you can! And, the enemy knows you can (which is why you are being fought). The question is: Do YOU know it?

 # DENYING SELF

NOTE TO SELF: "If the food show on the Travel Channel offends thee, cut it off. For it is better to enter into Heaven fit, than waddling and not able to enter through the pearly gates because of thy enormous girth."

 # BLESSINGS

I am learning to accept blessings that come by the hands of those who do not have the best/purest intentions. Please pray for me, because I despise pretentiousness, but I know God will make our enemies our footstools and that the wealth of the wicked is laid up for the just.

 # PUBLIC OPINION

Omonpee glad that she is not ruled or moved by people's opinion of her. What a harsh taskmaster public opinion can be!

CRUCIFYING FLESH

Crucifying of the flesh is an ongoing process. It requires a certain level of maturity and "want to." God does not do it all! We have to do our parts as well. But, we have to WANT TO. That's where trials and tribulations come in; they make us stronger, but, they are also used by God to develop the "want to" in us.
Thank God for the "want to."

LETTING GO

I've heard people say, "Never put a comma where God has put a period." I was meditating today and reflecting on this as it relates to FB and reconnecting with people. There is a REASON that exes are ex and the past has passed. Sometimes, we RECONNECT something that God Himself SEVERED; He KNEW that it would adversely affect our destiny! You cannot effectively go forward while looking backward.

ENABLING

Omonpee has repented for and is delivered from being an enabler! Enabling people DISABLED me for a time and a season; no more!

REVELATION: If, for me to be WHOLE, I have to CUT YOU OFF, then, love you, but, snip, snip.

19

Love, OWP

CASTING PEARLS

Omonpee has been delivered from casting pearls before swine. Believe it or not, I used to hunt people down to try to help them, only to find out that they did not really want change, but a temporary fix. Please learn from my mistakes and do not do this. No good comes from it. It is said that the Good Lord helps those who help themselves; me, too :-).

RESURRECTION

"And he said unto me, Son of man, can these bones live? And I answered, O Lord GOD, thou knowest."
- Ezekiel 37:3 KJV

God is a god of resurrection. I am thanking God because He is resurrecting some GOOD things in my life/personality that had been buried under some BAD things/experiences/relationships.
Thank you all for your continued prayers.

WINNERS/HATERS

"No weapon that is formed against thee shall prosper; and every tongue [that] shall rise against thee in judgment thou shalt condemn. This [is] the heritage of the servants of the LORD , and their righteousness [is] of me, saith the LORD." - Isaiah 54:17 KJV

REVELATION:
Winners don't HATE and HATERS DON'T WIN!!

20

LIGHT OF THE WORLD

"Ye are the light of the world. A city that is set on an hill cannot be hid." - Matthew 5:14 KJV

REVELATION: When there is greatness upon your life, do not try to dull your shine to stop people from being jealous or envious. It won't work any way.
Do you; be you!

THE GOOD OF THE LAND

REVELATION RECEIVED WHILE CLEANING 10 LBS. OF CHITTERLINGS TODAY :-) : If you want to "eat the good of the land," you must do away with mess in your life. Mess stinks and can be toxic! Get rid of the mess so that you will have only the best!

BLACKMAIL

REVELATION: Refuse to be blackmailed, especially emotionally. Do not allow the enemy to hold anything over you head. Recently, two relatives said things about me on FB that were either untrue or grossly exaggerated. As a minister, I help people get free; I will not be in bondage myself! The devil is a liar. A lie will not stand and "EVERY tongue that rises up against you in judgment YOU shall condemn."

Love, OWP

WHAT'S IN A NAME?

Contemplating names/nicknames/monikers I've been called by FB friends. Omonpee, 'Monpee, Pay, Pee, Pey, O.W., Opy, Prophetess, Woman of God, The Divine Ms. O., Ms. O, O, GG, Ms. Petcoff, Cuppy Cake, Omon, LBS.

I am glad to be so loved until people affectionately make up names for me. It reminds me of Jesus when He asked, "Whom do men say that I am?". :-) ♥ U all!

FRIES

"Dear Lord, please help the fry cook at our local McDonald's. Apparently, he either cannot see how much salt he is putting on the fries, or just likes them that shade of white. I understand that McDonald's uses Coke products. Maybe the man has the slogans mixed up and confused and that is why he does this. Please help him to see that the slogan is NOT, 'Have a STROKE and a smile!'. Amen."

STUDY

THE PROBLEM: "For I bear them record that they have a ZEAL (earnestly desiring to do something) of God, BUT NOT ACCORDING TO KNOWLEDGE." (Rom. 10:2). THE SOLUTION: "STUDY to shew thyself approved (equipped with knowledge and ready for service) unto God, a workman that needeth not to be ashamed, rightly dividing the word of truth." (II Tim. 2:15).

LIGHT OF THE WORLD

Repost from a dear FBF :
"People are like stained-glass windows. They sparkle and shine when the sun is out, but when the darkness sets in, their true beauty is revealed only if there is a light from within." - Elizabeth Kubler Ross

REVELATION: What's in you will come out; On the other hand, perpetrators will be exposed.

"Let your light so shine before men, that they may see your good works, and glorify your Father which is in heaven." - Matthew 5:16 KJV

BEING SURE

It is important that we KNOW who we are and what God has spoken to us about our life and our steps. When storms come, the only thing that we have to hold on to is what we are SURE of. It is what keeps us "grounded". What someone else has said to us does not always HOLD during the turbulent times. Formulating and maintaining a relationship with God for ourselves is the best insurance policy for the storms of life.

RESURRECTION

Omonpee is thanking God for the RESURRECTING power of His Word. HE spoke, and Lazarus ROSE (John 11:1-45). HE spoke, and the centurion's daughter ROSE (Luke 38:44). HE spoke and Omonpee ROSE!!
And, HE ROSE so that we can RISE.

23

 ## BEING LOVED

REVELATION WHILE WRITING: I am thankful that I KNOW that I am loved. (Everyday my husband - Ronald Petcoff - tells me he loves me and I am beautiful.) I am also thankful that I KNOW and LOVE myself. But, most of all I am thankful that I KNOW that God loves me. This KNOWLEDGE solidifies my self-esteem/self-confidence, imperfections and all.

Because I am LOVED, I can LOVE OTHERS; because I can LOVE OTHERS, I am LOVED in return. This is the an example of the Law of Reciprocation.

When we know who we are in Christ, it is the best feeling in the world! We do not need another person to complete us or to make us happy. I love my husband, but, if for some reason he were not in my life, I would still love me because I have learned to love myself through the eyes of Christ.

Also, though, when we base our happiness, self-esteem or self-worth on someone else's love for us, we put that person in the place in our life where God should be. We make an idol out of that person.

 ## POOR OSCAR

Omonpee is thinking, "I have at least two things in common with Oscar the Grouch: Both our first names begin with 'O' and we both need to do something with our eyebrows." :-)

STRANGE DREAMS

Omonpee woke up, angry, in full adrenaline rush. Mad at "Bobby" for being a ne'er-do-well mooch, trying to take the keys to my powder blue DeLorean! Problem(s): I do not know "Bobby", nor do I own a powder blue ANYTHING, especially a DeLorean.

Bobby & the DeLorean were products of hormone fluctuations; a horrible dream that has cost me precious rest time! Please check your thyroid. This has been a public service announcement LOL.

GOOD GIFTS

Ron and I went to a candy store today. I bought candy, including (only) 2 lemon & 2 orange wedges. Later, I offered Desmond "some" candy. Without hesitation, he took BOTH lemon wedges! I thought he would only take 1, but I didn't say a word and let him have them. REVELATION: Don't limit God! He NEVER told you you couldn't have MORE; that was your (and my) own thinking!

"If ye then, being evil, know how to give good gifts unto your children, how much more shall your Father which is in heaven give good things to them that ask him?" - Matthew 7:11 KJV

25

Love, OWP

WORD OF THE LORD

FELT LED TO POST: When you have a call of God on your life, your mere PRESENCE - nay, EXISTENCE - will make some people uncomfortable, for nothing that you have done but being you. You are not always going to fit in nor be accepted. You will be despised, rejected and persecuted. But, we have this hope; that if we suffer with Him, we will reign with Him. Do you, and watch Him show up and show out in your life.

PREPAREDNESS

REVELATION - Just because you really, really WANT to do something, does not mean that you are qualified to do it or do it well (especially and including ministry). If my 12-year-old son really, really wanted to drive my car, I would be a fool to give him the keys and tell him to go for it.

For one thing, he is not old/MATURE enough. For another thing, he does not KNOW HOW to drive.

There is a saying that says, "Anything worth doing is worth doing well." This should be especially true of things pertaining to ministry and things of the Lord. We owe Him our best. IF you are going to minister, BE PREPARED. Study, be equipped and live a lifestyle in which you can be instant, in season and out of season, to do the work of ministry.

 # BEING POLITE

The word "polite" comes from the Latin word, "politus", which means, "polished; made smooth." Society has taught us to be "polite" in our dealings with others, but, many times we are SMOOTHING OVER a bad or uncomfortable situation, POLISHING it, so that it looks better than it is. The Bible says that, "... the VIOLENT take it by force." (Matthew 11:12b). Sometimes, polite just doesn't work.

 # FIRST THINGS FIRST

REVELATION: A house is not built from the outside in, nor is it built from the top to the bottom. Foundation and "innards" MUST be first! That is a law of physics...and a spiritual law as well. We cannot win people to Christ by worrying about or judging them by their language, their clothing, their "habits". When the FOUNDATION is SOLID and the INSIDE is 'REMODELED", it will reflect on the OUTSIDE.

 # SPIRITUAL GIFTS

I am sitting here with what they tell me is some of the most cutting edge software/hardware needed to make videos and mp3s. BUT, I don't know how to use it fully; can't get this wonderful song that I made on Garage Band yesterday uploaded.

REVELATION: Spiritual gifts come "pre-installed" (are without repentance), but, without salvation and teaching and in the wrong hands, they are useless, frustrating or dangerous!

 ## NEW WINE

REVELATION FOR SOMEONE TODAY: Don't put new wine into old bottles (Luke 5:37-38). God said that you are not the person you used to be. You really didn't fit in with those people back then, but you CERTAINLY don't fit in with them now. God has had you hidden right out in the open all this time. They could not SEE who you were BECAUSE
HE WOULD NOT ALLOW IT!

 ## RELATIONSHIPS

Omonpee has changed. I am cutting off harmful, unproductive relationships. I am neither angry nor bitter. "It's just her hormones."; "She's crazy." No, I realize that it just ain't working. RELATIONSHIP involves RELATION. And RELATION involves RELATING. The Bible says, "How can two walk together except they be AGREED (able to RELATE in harmony)?"God is doing too much in me to let unproductive "unions" hinder it.

 ## INHIBITIONS

INHIBITIONS: After surgery & the hormones swinging, that "barrier" that kept me from saying or doing things that MIGHT hurt someone's feelings or offend them EVEN AT THE COST OF HURTING MYSELF had been compromised. But now I see this was a blessing in disguise! Not to purposely offend or hurt, but I am finding myself more able to say what I need to say. I am better able to protect God's Investment-ME!
Break through!

 # O-M-O-N-P-E-E

Posted by my friend Olivia Wallis Fletcher
(The other O.W.):
Omonpee:
O=Outrageous
M=Magnificent
O=Oh ,Wow(!)
N=Nice
P=Priceless
E=Enchanted
E=Enigmatic
x x x

Thanks, O.W! ♥ you!

 # "FLASH LIGHT"

" (JESUS,) the dayspring from on high hath visited us,
To give LIGHT to them that sit in darkness and [in] the
shadow of death to guide our feet into the way of
peace." - Luke 1:78c-79 KJV;

REVELATION: (If we choose to accept it) Everybody's
got a little LIGHT UNDER THE SON
(with apologies to George Clinton :-))!

Love, OWP

 ## SUPPORT

My neighbor had two dogs; one a big, quiet dog and the other, a small, yappy dog. Everyday, the small, yappy dog would stand in the yard next to the big, quiet dog and would BARK AND YAP at us, as if to say, "If I could get to you, I would tear you apart." The big, quiet dog died in December. The small yappy dog does not bark or yap anymore. He KNEW that his partner HAS HIS BACK before, but is now gone.

REVELATION: Know who's in your corner and on your side. Cherish and embrace them. They are few and far between.

 ## DELIVERY

PARABLE OF THE MISSING MAIL: I mailed someone something that should have taken 3-4 days to arrive. By day 10, no mail. I contemplated re-mailing TOMORROW - day 13. Today - day 12 (within HOURS of when I would have re-mailed) - the package arrived in good shape.

God said to tell you to NOT give up on your DELIVERY that He has promised. "At an hour in which you think not", it WILL show up!

WORD: RESTORATION

REVELATION: God said to tell you that there are some things that you have counted LOST FOREVER, that, because of you OBEDIENCE to Him, He will RESTORE. They weren't lost; they were HIDDEN for "such a time as this." THIS IS YOUR SEASON TO HAVE THE HIDDEN THINGS REVEALED.

LOVE POWER

"There is no fear in love; but perfect love casteth out fear: because fear hath torment. He that feareth is not made perfect in love." - I John 4:18 KJV

REVELATION:
"We've got LOVE POWER;
It's the GREATEST POWER of them all.
We've got LOVE POWER
And together [with God] we can't fall."
(Luther Vandross)

CONFINED SPACES

Omonpee is working on her new book cover, using a HIGH QUALITY (LOTS OF DPI/PIXELS) pic of herself, made to print at 8x10, "squishing" it into a MUCH SMALLER SPACE. Result? FRUSTRATION, because the pic DISTORTS so small; her EYES look COCKED :-).

REVELATION - Never let ANYONE SQUISH you into a place that you don't fit/have outgrown, changing YOU to "FIT" THEIR NEEDS/DESIRES. Be YOU in all of your "GLORY", as God intended.

Love, OWP

 # DREAMS

Be mindful of what you share and with whom.
Dreams in infancy must be protected.

 # ADVOCATE

Omonpee is a Desmondologist. I know all about my
son, what makes him tick and am the best ADVOCATE
(in terms of the school/education system) he could ever
possibly have. This is because I love him and have
STUDIED him, top to bottom, inside and out.

REVELATION: God is a YOU-ologist! He loves us so
much until He knows the number of hairs on our head.
He sent His Son Jesus to be an ADVOCATE;
a MEDIATOR between God and Man.

 # WISE MINISTRY

Proverbs 11:30 says, "He that winneth souls is WISE."
WISE! What is WISE about beating people over the
head, trying to MAKE them see your point of view,
judging them; being concerned about them SOUNDING
or LOOKING "HOLY" rather than TEACHING them
THROUGH A LIVING EXAMPLE the way of
SANCTIFICATION?
I didn't even need a REVELATION to see that that is not
going to work and is not of God.

 *LET IT GO*

Omonpee just got a revelation of, "Be angry, but sin not". I no longer stew on things. For one thing, my health won't allow it. But, for another (the most important) thing, when I allow people to anger me to the brewing point, my "insides" pay the price. My body is the Temple of the Lord; allowing it to get "messed up" because of anger is a SIN. In the words of Mase, "Breathe, stretch, shake, LET IT GO!".

 *HIDDEN THINGS*

Omonpee just found 2 pair of earrings that she thought she lost three to four years ago during a ministry trip to Delaware! These earrings were black spinel that I had made and onyx) and were in a pouch in the overnight kit all these years. We have used that kit several times since then. I found them being obedient to the Holy Spirit when it told me to get up and get dressed for Mother's Day dinner with Desmond.

REVELATION: God said to tell you that there are some things that you have counted LOST FOREVER, that, because of you OBEDIENCE to Him, He will RESTORE. They weren't lost; they were HIDDEN for "such a time as this." THIS IS YOUR SEASON TO HAVE THE HIDDEN THINGS REVEALED.

Love, OWP

 ## "DIFFERENT"

Body of Christ, I implore us to please not overlook or cast aside blessings and/or people just because they don't come wrapped like we think they should. I have met WONDERFUL people on FB, some that are "colorful", "mouthy", not "churchy" at all ☺,but God has used them to bless me tremendously and has used me in their lives as well.

I ♥ them ...and, unlike some church folks, they GENUINELY ♥ me!

He that hath ears to hear...

 ## AWAKENING

God had been trying to get my attention about this book writing and all I have had to do for quite some time. I am reminded of an old NyQuil commercial where the couple was lying in bed, and the one woke the other up sick and coughing:

After the cancer diagnosis this past year and all the other "hell" I have been through, when He asked, "Prophet, are you UP?", you could not beat me answering,
"I'M UP NOW!" LOL

 # FRIEND LIST

REVELATION: On Judgment Day, there will be a lot of people who will try to get on God's Friend list at the last minute or who thought they "had it like that" because of their "STATUS." They will soon find out, though, that their request will be Ignored. He will say, "Depart from me, you worker of iniquity, I know you not."

 # LAZARUS, COME FORTH

Readers of "The Chronicles of Petcoff" may recall that, last year this time, our heroine converted her spare bedroom into her isolation room (used for radioactive iodine treatment). Later, she converted the same room into her office. In medias res (i.e.," meanwhile back at the ranch"), she found isolation clothing in the closet today. God spoke, "Lazarus, rise & shed your grave clothes" to her spirit; she became verklempt.

 # RECEIVE THE BLESSING

I am learning to RECEIVE blessings without hesitation, consternation and/or deliberation. This is a cause for celebration, even despite the hateration. The blessings are coming in groves, and while that is an idiom, it is no exaggeration :-).

 ## BASKETS

Ron called from work last night to say that work was throwing out SEVERAL nice large wicker baskets, all shapes and sizes. He told me he was bringing them home. There were breadbaskets, fruit baskets and very large and very nice baskets with linings in them (for some reason there were marked "LAUNDRY", but, I would never use them for that - TOO NICE).

REVELATION: In the Bible, baskets represent increase and abundant supply usually from a reaped harvest or its by-products! We have SOWN and SOWN for year and have now stepped into our season of supernatural increase and reaping!

 ## A REAL BLESSING

Omonpee heard this in her spirit while grocery shopping: "The blessing of the Lord, it maketh rich, and he addeth no sorrow with it. "(Proverbs 10:22 KJV)

If there is sorrow with it, then it is not a blessing of the Lord, even if it makes you "rich." But, if it is a blessing of the Lord, do not allow anything or anybody to make you sorry for receiving it. Embrace it, sit back and watch God do His Thing in your life."

 *Focus*

When you are completely sold out to the Lord, your life is no longer your own. Your focus is not on tradition, perceived/expected familial relationships or responsibilities, other people's expectations of what your actions should be or how your life should've/would've/could've been. Your focus is on the ASSIGNMENT that God has for your life....

You no longer have "a life" as others do, because you have "lost it" to FIND the one that is HIDDEN in Him. You have chosen to live your life to please GOD and not to please MAN.

There is much power and peace that come when full acceptance of this takes place in mind of this type of Believer. The bondages of bonds can no longer be used by the enemy to keep you from doing what you are called to do. "Who is my mother and my brother? Them that do the will of my Father." You align yourself with people to whom God has aligned you, and, whenever that season is up, you are not moved or stagnated by the ending of that season, but, because your focus is on God's Will for your life, you go on to your next assignment.

He that hath an ear to hear…

Love, OWP

HANDLING VIPERS

REPOST FROM A DEAR FBF, WITH A
TWIST OF MY OWN:

Acts 28:3-5 - Paul got bitten by a snake. Paul knew who
he was in God. He shook the snake into the fire and
kept going, TOTALLY UNHARMED. The people
looking on became Believers.

REVELATION: People are watching YOU to see how
you handle VIPERS in your life. WHEN YOU KNOW
WHO YOU ARE IN CHRIST, you can shake OFF the
vipers and keep going.

And, the VIPERS get burned in the FIRE!
Our God is a consuming fire!

You can go through things that were designed by the
enemy and the people he uses to KILL you - kill you
physically, kill your character, kill your spirit. But,
when you KNOW who you are in Christ and you have
His Authority and His Word, you have the POWER to
shake these things off.

2011

STATUSES

HEAD BANGERS

FACT (FROM MY HUSBAND'S COPY OF "SMITHSONIAN" MAGAZINE): A "woodpecker" can "REPEATEDLY BAND ITS HEAD INTO A TREE 15 miles per hour WITHOUT harming itself."

REVELATION (FROM THE HOLY GHOST): YOU - A HUMAN - CANNOT! Stop REPEATEDLY BANGING YOUR HEAD over the same problem/situation! Pray over it, do what God told you to do, and leave the rest to Him.

LIGHT BURDENS

God's Gifts/Callings are not intended to be a curse. His Yoke is EASY; His Burdens are LIGHT. Therefore, it is never HIM, but how WE facilitate what He has given us to do. (If I am struggling or stressing, I could be trying to do some things that I don't have grace for or are not my assignment.)

KINGDOM WORK

Omonpee has been getting these CastleVille notifications on her wall that read, "_____ (person's name) GOT BUSY in YOUR KINGDOM!" I don't play CastleVille (Desmond did, but not lately), and don't care about THAT KINGDOM. However.... when I stand before GOD on Judgment Day, I SURE DO WANT TO HEAR GOD SAY THAT ABOUT OMONPEE and HIS KINGDOM! "Girl, you GOT BUSY in MY KINGDOM! WELL DONE, MY GOOD AND FAITHFUL SERVANT!" Glory!!

39

SNAKES/SERPENTS

REVELATION OF THE SNAKES/SERPENT

"THEY SHALL TAKE UP SERPENTS; and if they drink any deadly thing, it shall not hurt them; they shall lay hands on the sick, and they shall recover."
- Mark 16:18 KJV

Paul gathered a pile of brushwood and, as he put it on the fire, A VIPER, driven out by the heat, FASTENED ITSELF ONTO HIS HAND.

But Paul SHOOK THE SNAKE OFF into the fire and SUFFERED NO ILL EFFECTS. - Acts 28:5

God said that there is someone who is and has been for a while now going through RELATIONSHIPS with unsavory people :-). The person(s) has/have proven time and time again that they cannot be trusted and have VIPEROUS AGENDAS toward you. You have prayed to God and asked, "WHY do I have to keep putting myself in a position to be HURT by this person/these people?/WHY do I HAVE TO KEEP FOOLING WITH THIS SITUATION?; HOW LONG, LORD?" You are in turmoil and are even losing sleep over this (even and especially during this holiday season). (I know you are because God WOKE ME UP OUT OF MY NICE, WARM BED AT 5:41 a.m. to share this with you :-)).

GOD SAID that He is TRAINING YOU TO HANDLE SNAKES. The word "hurt" in the Mark 16:18 KJV reference comes from the Greek word blaptō, which means "hurt/harm/injure". It is NOT the same as NOT BEING ABLE TO FEEL THE IMPACT ("Ouch! That hurt."). Instead, *blaptō* means not having an ill/lasting effect on you. God said that He has allowed you to learn to FEEL the IMPACT of the SNAKE BITES to STRENGTHEN YOU FOR THE NEXT ONES and to BUILD UP A SPIRITUAL ANTIBODY against such! What would KILL OTHERS will come to be SECOND NATURE TO YOU because He has allowed you to go through it so often and so long. Like Paul, you will grow to the point where you will NO LONGER BE MOVED BY THE VIPERS, but will continue to MINISTER/DO WHAT GOD HAS CALLED YOU TO DO without MISSING A BEAT and actually INCORPORATE the VIPER BITING as part of "the act" :-), being a LIVING, BREATHING testimony that one CAN survive being "bitten" and keep right on trucking (You shall NOT surely die, but LIVE AND DECLARE THE WORKS OF THE LORD!).

HOW I GOT OVER

My SOUL looks back and WONDERS HOW I GOT OVER! But, my SPIRIT REMEMBERS and BEARS WITNESS that it was only THROUGH JESUS! Glory!!

LOOKIN' GOOD

Omonpee is sitting here reflecting (again; must be the season) and is THANKFUL that she DOESN'T LOOK LIKE what she's BEEN THROUGH (or, at least, not most days, anyway :-)).

41

Love, OWP

 ## MOTIVES

"Ye ask, and receive not, because ye ask amiss, that ye may consume [it] upon your lusts."- James 4:3 KJV

REVELATION - We must be mindful of our MOTIVES for wanting "stuff" (money, possession, positions, promotions, titles). Do you want it because somebody else has it? Do you want it because it will make you feel "important"? What would you do with it, once you got it? Would you use it to edify and build the Kingdom of God, help mankind, make the world better, etc.? Or, would you HOARD it and waste it, just to say you have it? When we purge ourselves of selfish motives, we will see more of our prayers being answered. We will not be so FRUSTRATED SPIRITUALLY and will be more EFFECTIVE in Kingdom work.

 ## SEEK HIM EARLY

There was/is a reason why David decreed, "EARLY will I SEEK THEE..."(Psalm 63:1). There is POWER in making the worship of God the FIRST THING you do in the morning and the LAST THING you do at night (Isaiah 26:9). It CONDITIONS you and PREPARES YOUR MIND to keep stayed on Him. Reflecting on some things I have recently experienced, had I NOT taken the time to have been in PRAYER, MEDITATION, AND REFLECTION IN THE WORD, it would not have been nice; thank God for His Keeping Power that was reinforced through our teachings in our early morning family Bible study and bedtime Bible recitations.

 ## Auto Correct

AUTO CORRECT CAN BE A MESS :-)! - I don't use a cell phone for FB, but I constantly read comments from people who do about how the auto-correct features "help" them a little too much by "correcting" and "changing" a word just because AUTO-CORRECT "THINKS" it knows what the person MEANT to say, based on what AUTO-CORRECT BELIEVES the PERSON SHOULD HAVE MEANT! Oftentimes, the person ends up having to go back behind Auto-correct to correct it :-)!

REVELATION - Again (been in this vein since last night), we must be careful from whom we receive COUNSEL. EXCEPT THEY SEE BY THE HOLY SPIRIT, they do not REALLY KNOW. They do not know WHO YOU ARE, WHAT GOD SAID TO YOU, WHAT YOUR REAL INTENTIONS ARE/PURPOSE IS for doing x-y-z in your life! They may be trying to correct something that LOOKS LIKE A MISTAKE TO THEM based on what God would say to THEM about THEIR OWN LIFE. But, whatever you are doing/going through/planning may be EXACTLY THE WAY GOD INTENDED IT FOR YOU! If you ACCEPT that erroneous correction, you will oftentimes end up in a MESS and without the ASSURANCE of the backing of God on that decision, because you are now OUT OF HIS WILL. Your life/ministry will not have "said" what God intended for it to say/do/accomplish.

Love, OWP

RECEIVING COUNSEL

We must be careful of the counsel we receive. No matter how well-intentioned or anointed the person is, he or she was not there when God spoke to YOU concerning YOU and your assignment. Listen with a teachable spirit and always be ready to receive Godly correction, admonishment, rebuke and reproof...BUT... remember that EVERY MAN must work out HIS SALVATION with FEAR AND TREMBLING. If what the "counselor" is telling you is CONTRARY to what you KNOW GOD IS SAYING/HAS SAID, do not follow the human!
Well-intentioned people can unwittingly "counsel" you right out of your destiny!

PROJECTING GOD

REVELATION - "God"/The Name of God does not appear ANYWHERE within The Book of Esther...YET this book contains INVALUABLE SPIRITUAL REVELATION because we can GLEAN from: (1) Esther's GODLY/DIVINELY-DIRECTED ACTIONS and (2) the GODLY-INSPIRED CONCLUSION that God's Hand was DEFINITELY upon Esther and that He DIRECTED HER by giving her SPECIFIC INSTRUCTIONS, TACTICS AND STRATEGY. God said that we do not always have to yell, "GOD THIS/GOD THAT" to be ministering. People OUGHT TO be able to LOOK AT OUR ACTIONS and SEE GOD'S HAND AT WORK IN US AND THROUGH US and through OUR FRUIT.

WORD: SINGLE WOMEN

JUST HEARD THIS IN MY SPIRIT WHILE COMING HOME FROM LUNCH WITH MY HUSBAND: Single/Unmarried Woman of God, just because God has not sent you A MAN does not mean that He cannot/will not send you MAN-NA (manna)! GOD IS YOUR PROVIDER!

ALL MUSHED UP

But for His Grace - But for the fact that He loved me enough to BREAK ME into tiny, little, pieces and then MUSH those pieces into something PLIABLE, so that I could be used by Him - I stood a GOOD CHANCE be a HOT, ARROGANT, HAUGHTY mess! Y'all wouldn't have wanted to BE AROUND ME, let alone TALK TO ME. Oh, but for HIS GRACE...
I've been MUSHED, y'all ☺.

LET US PRAY

WORD FOR THE DAY: Let us pray.

PEACE

Omonpee is reflective this morning and is thankful for where He brought her from, spiritually, emotionally and psychologically. She may not live in MAYBERRY with ANDY and OPEE, but she thanks God she does not reside on ELM STREET with FREDDY. Glory! Thank God for the PEACE that SURPASSES ALL UNDERSTANDING!!

BEDTIME POEM #1

Now I lay me down; Bye, bye!
Electric blanket set to High.

Meds are taken; prayers are said.
"That Boy" has been long sent off to bed!

Nestled up in the mattress, three layers deep…
Oh, no! Now I can't go to sleep ☹!!

Perhaps a Word Find or two
Will help me drift off in just a few?!?

Back out of the bed to hunt up the stuff,
Two puzzles; one pencils? Yeah, that's enough.

Back into the bed I go
(Ron is amused by my "Time to Sleep" show ☺.)

On second thought….
If I should cry while trying to dream,
I rolled over on a pencil and am trying not to scream

And wake the house with my loud noises!
No, on second thought, I'll make different choices

And just MAKE MYSELF lie down and rest.
To sleep, I will surely do my best!

Good night, Facebook! Sleep well, 'cause I'm gonna!
God willing, I'll see you all in the manana.

TRUSTING FOR REST

Can you TRUST GOD ENOUGH to REST? Resting says, "Lord, I have done all that you have told me to do and I must now put this in Your Hands while I REFUEL this BODY and this SPIRIT that You gave me so that I can CONTINUE to follow FURTHER INSTRUCTIONS. In RESTING, I TRUST YOU to HANDLE ALL THAT CONCERNS ME during this time that I CANNOT BECAUSE I AM RECHARGING/RE-FILLING."

GO WITH THE FLOW

REVELATION FOR THE MATURE: When God tells you to do something, you do not necessarily always need to know WHY...Just DO WHAT HE TOLD YOU TO DO! Knowing "WHY" may satiate the human appetite for logic, but is really immaterial; either you are going to do it or you are not. Either you are going to trust Him or you are not. When He speaks, you do: GO WITH THE FLOW.

BEING "INSURED"

REVELATION: God's DIVINE INSTRUCTION to us - i.e., what He TOLD YOU/DIRECTED YOU TO DO/SAY - is our "INSURANCE POLICY" against (SPIRITUAL) "MAYHEM" (think Allstate commercials). When we OPERATE outside of the realm of His Instruction, we are "UNINSURED OPERATORS." At that point, we are not covered!

Love, OWP

SEASON OF LACK

HEARD THIS IN MY SPIRIT - There is somebody who is experiencing a SEASON OF LACK right now. God was showing me how, in my OWN LIFE, while the SEASON OF LACK was certainly UNCOMFORTABLE, it caused me to SEEK GOD in an entirely different dimension. DIMENSIONS OF FAITH AND GRACE were revealed to me that I would never have EXPERIENCED had I not "lacked."

The Bible says that He will make our feet like hindsfeet; those feet can walk on steep, twisted, narrow mountain cliffs and peaks and NEVER MISS A STEP. I see in the spirit a TIGHTROPE WALKER, whose skills have been honed to walk the tightrope and NEVER misstep. God is showing me that when you go through these SEASONS OF LACK when things are really "tight", when you enter into deeper dimensions of FAITH AND GRACE, you can STEP and not miss.

What would KILL OTHERS who have "always had, and don't understand WHY you don't" becomes common place to you. God will then use you to teach those others in their time of LACK.

NO OTHER GODS

Whenever we base our feelings of SECURITY on what we have, we are putting those things in the place in our lives where God should be.
He will have no other gods before Him.

SUCCESSFUL MINISTRY

HEARD THIS IN MY SPIRIT JUST NOW - Your ministry is NOT for everybody! It is only for those to whom God has assigned you and to whom you have been assigned. "Bigger" is not always better and does not always mean more successful. You do not have GRACE to pastor/lead/even minister to those to whom you are NOT ASSIGNED ("DEEP FOLKS" - "SOME plant, SOME water, BUT GOD GIVES THE INCREASE"). Some of the warfare you have in your ministry/church may be because there are people there who should not be; who belong elsewhere. As God replants them, let them go with love. It is best for all involved. Be faithful in SERVING those who ARE assigned to you; that is TRUE SUCCESS.

"DEEP"

Real DEEP doesn't act "deep." (Don't believe me? Jesus taught in parables and ate with publicans and sinners.)

LIGHT, BE!

"Light, BE!" - (Original translation of) Gen. 1:3 KJV;

REVELATION - When you speak with AUTHORITY and POWER, you don't have to SAY MANY WORDS to GET THE JOB DONE/THE POINT ACROSS! Speak THE WORD OF GOD with AUTHORITY AND ASSURANCE (IN FAITH)...and then STEP BACK and WATCH GOD WORK!

Love, OWP

SELFLESSNESS

"Wherefore, if meat make my brother to offend, I will eat no flesh while the world standeth, lest I make my brother to offend." - I Cor. 8:13 KJV (Oxford)

REVELATION - Many Christians say that they would GIVE UP THEIR LIVES for the sake of the Gospel, but how many would give up their QUARTER POUNDER WITH CHEESE? Their WHOPPER? Their DOUBLE DOUBLE? For the REST OF THEIR LIVES????? The Love of Christ COMPELS one to SERVE with their whole heart, mind and soul. There is a SELFLESSNESS that is developed with SPIRITUAL MATURITY in which the innate desires for SELF-PRESERVATION and SELF-SATISFACTION yield to the PASSION of seeing SOULS SAVED, people SET FREE, DELIVERED and EQUIPPED for KINGDOM OF GOD WORK.

DWELLING

"Finally, brethren, whatsoever things are true, whatsoever things are honest, whatsoever things are just, whatsoever things are pure, whatsoever things are lovely, whatsoever things are of good report; if there be any virtue, and if there be any praise, think on these things. " - Phil. 4:8 KJV

REVELATION - Oftentimes, we DWELL on the wrong things. DWELL on the RIGHT THINGS so that the enemy does not have leeway to TORMENT your mind with thoughts of painful experiences, past failures, embarrassments, doubt, etc.

50

ERRONEOUS ANSWERS

I was helping Desmond to study for a Biology test the other day; the teacher sent home a study sheet with multiple-choice questions. God gave me strategy to help Desmond: I took a black Sharpie and blacked out all of the WRONG answers so that when he studied, he would ONLY CONCENTRATE ON THE RIGHT ANSWERS. The WRONG ANSWER is IRRELEVANT as long as you know what the RIGHT ANSWER is. It eliminated the distraction of all the other ERRONEOUS words AND it helped ingrain in him what the right answer was. Then, when he took the test, no matter in what order the questions appear and no matter what OTHER WRONG ANSWERS may or may not have been thrown in to try to throw the students' off, HE COULD IDENTIFY AND CHOOSE THE RIGHT ANSWERS. He took the test and passed with flying colors.

REVELATION - God said to STOP FOCUSING ON THE WRONG ANSWER and SET YOUR FACE LIKE FLINT on the RIGHT ANSWER. Once you KNOW what God has said TO YOU, ABOUT YOU, FOR YOU, you KNOW the RIGHT ANSWER; you KNOW how the STORY ENDS. Stop allowing all the MULTIPLE CHOICES of WRONG ANSWERS (listening to people who don't really know; living in fear, etc.) to cloud your mind and influence your living. Entertaining wrong answers wastes times and will eventually get you off track.

Love, OWP

 ## MOVE THAT BUS!

I was flipping through channels and came across, "Extreme Home Makeover." The Lord showed me that, as badly as those people NEEDED that house and as much as they KNEW their newly renovated house was WAITING ON THEM, they COULD NOT GET TO IT until the COMMAND was given to, "MOVE THAT BUS!"

REVELATION: God said there are some of US who have STUFF waiting on US; we can see a glimpse of it, we can almost smell, taste and touch it...BUT...WE HAVE A "BUS" IN THE WAY! SOMETHING is blocking our ACCESS; our COMPLETE VIEW! In the Name of Jesus, SPEAK TO THE "BUS" and MOVE IT OUT OF THE WAY! MOVE THAT BUS to GET TO YOUR STUFF!

(And, for the "deep folks", "For verily I say unto you, That whosoever shall SAY UNTO THIS MOUNTAIN (bus, whatever), Be thou removed, and be thou cast into the sea; and shall not doubt in his heart, but shall believe that those things which he saith shall come to pass; HE SHALL HAVE WHATSOEVER HE SAITH." - MARK 11:23 KJV)

 ## CHOICE

Just because I don't, doesn't mean that I can't, nor that I don't know how or that I forgot. It just means that I CHOOSE NOT to.

 **DISCERNMENT**

The spiritual skills of RIGHTLY DISCERNING and RIGHTLY DIVIDING while in the midst of PAIN - PHYSICAL, SPIRITUAL, EMOTIONAL OR OTHERWISE - is one that is mastered and demonstrated by the SPIRITUALLY MATURE. To be able to "PARTITION OFF" (in computer terms, as the hard drive is the mind of the computer) your CURRENT "PAINFUL" state of mind from WHAT GOD WOULD SAY TO YOU ABOUT SOMETHING OR SOMEONE requires DISCIPLINE. Truthfully, as we become more MATURE (from "glory to glory; faith to faith") THE OLD MAN DIES; even if pain is present, THE VOICE OF THE NEW MAN IS MORE PRONOUNCED AND INFLUENTIAL in our lives.

Just because you are in pain in one area of your life does not mean that everybody and everything are out to get you at that moment (on the other hand, though, the enemy DOES like to strike when we are down, so that we must not be UNAWARE, busy tending to our "PAINS"). Looking through the EYES OF THE HOLY SPIRIT instead of through PHYSICAL EYES allows us to DISCERN the TIMES (even and especially in our own lives). The ability to do this is, indeed, the mark of one who is SPIRITUALLY MATURE and DISCIPLINED.

Love, OWP

WORD: MATRIARCHS

JUST HEARD THIS IN MY SPIRIT WITH INSTRUCTIONS TO POST IMMEDIATELY: Ladies, YOU are the MATRIARCH of YOUR HOUSE/HOUSEHOLD. Don't allow ANYBODY - Mamma, Mamma-in-Law, Daddy, Child, Friendgirl, Cuz, Oprah, Dr. Phil - to DICTATE to you what you should allow, how you handle your family, what you cook, how you decorate your house, how you raise your kids nor how you "wife" your husband. Pray and seek GOD for wisdom and HE will either speak to you directly, show you, or send someone TO HELP YOU (but NOT to take over). If they cannot respect YOU as the MATRIARCH of your house, CUT THEM OFF. That is YOUR marriage; YOUR children; YOUR life; not anyone else's.

GROW AND GO!

My daughter is grown up and gone and my son is, to my surprise, maturing quickly before my eyes. Because of this, I can FEEL some of the WEIGHT coming off; my son - for whom I have had to "think" a large part of his life - is now helping ME out in the thinking-ahead/rationalizing department. It is QUITE REWARDING. I was thinking of this in terms of PASTORS and MEMBERS; I don't pastor, but I imagine that the WEIGHT of taking care of OVERGROWN FOLKS has burned out a many of them. Grow up and get out, Church People! Too much work to be done!!

WORD: PROPHETS

JUST HEARD THIS IN MY SPIRIT - Be careful of making a "Word-for-the-nations" out of an INDIVIDUAL PROPHECY, with YOU being the INDIVIDUAL to whom the word is directed. This is a common mistake made by either IMMATURE prophets or people who simply don't want to hear anything negative about themselves. There are a lot of spiritually farsighted "prophets" who can SEE up in everybody else's lives but can't see when it comes to what God is showing THEM ABOUT THEM, particularly when He is showing them their shortcomings.

PEEPING TOMS

REVELATION: Too many spiritual PEEPING TOMS, trying to PEER into your HOUSE when they need to be WASHING THEIR OWN WINDOWS! They "get their jollies" watching YOU to see if you are going to SLIP UP and give them a show. When God said, "WATCHMEN ON THE WALL", He did not mean to monitor people's FB wall for foolishness. When people are WATCHING YOU (and they are), be FOUND doing THE WORK OF THE LORD!

ONE-UPMANSHIP

Lord, please deliver your people from the spirit of one-upmanship. If I tell you I have an in-grown toe nail, you tell me you have two, and had yours FIRST - and one has glitter on it. Help, Lord!

 ## HEAT WAVE

It had been over 100 F here for so long until now when I go out....AND IT IS IN THE 90'S...I consider that COOL! And, seriously, without a thermometer, I can tell the DIFFERENCE! What would have been HOT to me "back home" or even a few years ago here, is not only TOLERABLE but PLEASANT; A WELCOME CHANGE FROM THE SCORCHING HEAT we got used to recently.

REVELATION: God said that ALL THE HELL you have been through recently HAS PREPARED/IS PREPARING YOU to go through LESSER TRIALS....AND NOT BE MOVED. In fact, some of you even now are in something that is a CAKEWALK compared to "THAT OTHER THING" that you went through. The HELL on earth CONDITIONED YOU; it REFINED YOU; it PURGED YOU; it TOUGHENED YOU UP so that you will be/are able to KEEP YOUR COOL when others who have not been through what you have been through would MELT/FALL OUT/HAVE A SPIRITUAL HEATSTROKE. Thank God for the heat!

"Beloved, think it not strange concerning the FIERY TRIAL which is to try you, as though some strange thing happened unto you:

But REJOICE, inasmuch as ye are partakers of Christ's sufferings; that, when his glory shall be revealed, YE MAY BE GLAD ALSO WITH EXCEEDING JOY."
– I Peter 4:12-13 KJV

INTENT TO DEFRAUD

DID YOU KNOW that when you go to a Man or Woman of God with the INTENT to DECEIVE/TRICK/DEFRAUD THEM into praying over/counseling over/speaking over some MESS DISGUISED AS A PROBLEM that you are, in fact, COHORTING WITH THE ENEMY to try to trick GOD into saying what YOU WANT HIM TO SAY or DO WHAT YOU WANT HIM TO DO? Ask Ananias and Sapphira how that works out for you. **theme music to NBC's "The More You Know" segments plays here**

EXPLAINING YOURSELF

Stop trying to convince CARNAL PEOPLE of SPIRITUAL REVELATION. Stop trying to explain your spiritual self to carnal-minded folks. There are things that God will require YOU to do in FAITH. Mamma, Daddy, Sister, Brother, Uncle, Cuddin' Ray and 'nem...if they are not hearing what you are hearing, they cannot see what you are seeing. Stop trying to get them to see it your way; they will see soon enough by the MANIFESTATIONS of your OBEDIENCE to what God said to YOU.

SOUND COUNSEL

Omonpee, as a rule, does not seek counsel from many people on important spiritual matters. We must know to whom we are connected and assigned and who is assigned to us. Everybody does not have "a word" for us, nor the answers we need, no matter how well meaning they may be.

Love, OWP

WORD: DISTRACTIONS

HEARD THIS IN MY SPIRIT JUST NOW: The enemy will send DISTRACTIONS, sometimes in the form of people supposedly needing YOUR help. These distractions are to get you off task from doing something that is GERMANE to your DESTINY. You must use WISDOM and don't be afraid to say NO. Be like Nehemiah (Neh. 6:3) when people came to him while he was repairing the wall: "And I sent messengers unto them, saying, I am doing a great work, so that I cannot come down: why should the work cease, whilst I leave it, and come down to you?"

SMALL BUT IMPORTANT

While I was reflecting on how the absence of my thyroid - a seemingly SMALL, INSIGNIFICANT, UNSEEN gland has wreaked ALL MANOR OF CHAOS for me health-wise (I claim my healing in the Name of Jesus) - the Lord spoke to me and told me that there are MANY MINISTRIES/CHURCHES that are not functioning at their FULL POTENTIAL all because the LEADERS MESSED OVER and RAN OFF the SEEMINGLY SMALL, INSIGNIFICANT, UNSEEN MEMBERS!

STUDY TO BE QUIET

Study to be quiet. Seriously.

DISSENSION IN BODY

I had worked so hard to get all four computers networked with all three printers. At onset, it all worked. Today, however, I noticed DISSENSION in the network. The Canon won't RECOGNIZE the iMac, etc., but all computers will PRINT to all PRINTERS if "forced." I have developed a work around, but it has sent me running back and forth all over the house today; NETWORKING was supposed to eliminate that very thing. This decreased my PRODUCTIVITY.

At a time when I should be GETTING SOME WORK DONE, I am finding a way ("Who's on first?") to make sure that this one talks to that one or working around this one who is not speaking to the other one.

The Lord showed me a parallel between this and the church. Glean from it what revelation you will; I'd spell it out, but I have lost time today and have to get back to work ☺.

DIVINE "MISTAKES"

When you obey God, what you THINK looks like a MISTAKE or a MISSTEP is actually His Divine Hand working in a situation. His Thoughts are not our thoughts; His Ways are not our ways. That is why what may look wrong or weird to us, IF HE ORCHESTRATED IT; BLESSED IT, ORDAINED IT, it will turn out better than we could imagine. It takes only FAITH and DOING (WORKS) on our part. Faith without works is dead and understanding is not required.

59

Love, OWP

WORD: EXPECTATIONS

HEARD THIS IN MY SPIRIT FOR SOMEONE - You cannot change a person. If you keep getting hurt by a person it is YOU who must change; you must change your EXPECTATIONS of the person.

HANDLING SOULS

When you view the people on your Friend list as SOULS rather than mere "FBFs" (with the perception being "friends" versus true friends), it changes your perception of how you handle people. At that point, it is not about adding to the number of people on your list; with each person comes a Kingdom responsibility to minister; to handle with love and Godly care.

"If I, even I, be lifted up, I'll draw all men unto me."

THE ULTIMATE HACKER

Omonpee is reading the posts where people have gotten hacked by that spider video and is thinking about how hackers prey on our human curiosity. Not the spider, but THE SERPENT - Satan - was the ULTIMATE HACKER.

He preyed upon this same curiosity with EVE and ADAM in the Garden of Eden; they HAD TO KNOW what that fruit tasted like. Satan HACKED INTO our standing as SINLESS BEINGS at that point, INFESTING humanity with the VIRUS OF SIN. It would take JESUS to come in and "clean it up."

WORD: PUBLIC OPINION

HEARD IN MY SPIRIT DURING MEDITATION THIS MORNING - Never allow public opinion - ACCEPTANCE NOR REJECTION - to be a barometer for the success of your ministry or the success of your life. A crowd yelled, "Hosanna, Hosanna" at the beginning of Jesus' Ministry; some of that very same crowd yelled, "CRUCIFY HIM!" toward the end of His Life.

MINISTER AVAILABILITY

Some non-Catholic Christian ministers have problems with Catholicism and people having to go through the priest to reach God (I, too, believe that Jesus is the mediator between God and man, not the priest). Yet, some of these same ministers are THEMSELVES UNAVAILABLE/UNAPPROACHABLE to the PEOPLE. Are you better than God Himself?

I understand that there are only so many hours in the day, etc., and one person can only do so much. But, a shepherd who does not like sheep/handling sheep is really in the wrong line of work.

"IMPORTANT" ONES

It both tickles and vexes me (yes, I am strange like that ☺) that a lot of preachers - on FB and otherwise - try to sound soooo "IMPORTANT" but are really SPIRITUALLY IMPOTENT. Talkin' loud and saying nothing. Try the spirit by the spirit when you are hearing/reading to discern WHAT - IF ANYTHING AT ALL - of substance is being said.

61

FAITHFUL OVER A FEW

People always want (what they perceive to be) some "GREAT COMMANDMENT" from the Lord. Yet, they don't (want to) obey the in "the small things." How are you going to pastor a MEGACHURCH when you can't be faithful to TEACH/PREACH TO and MEET THE NEEDS of 5-6 people or even those in your HOUSEHOLD? If you CANNOT (CHOOSE NOT TO) be faithful OVER A FEW, you need not expect to "RULE" SUCCESSFULLY OVER THE MANY.

FAITH WITHOUT WORKS

It does not say that man does not need BREAD, only that he also needs "every word that proceeds out of the mouth of God." We are spiritual beings that live in a physical body...but we do live in a body! We have to feed the SPIRIT of a person AS WELL AS take care of the physical needs. And for those who say otherwise, if you are so SPIRITUAL, stop EATING AND DRINKING FOREVER and see where it gets you. If it is not good enough for YOU, then why would it be good enough for those in NEED?

Every need is not met with prayer alone; some involves some "Do-something" on our parts. Sometimes, in the time that it takes to tell people with a pressing need, "I'll pray for you" we could have gone into our purses and pulled out some money to pay a bill, cooked a meal to feed a family or sat down and listened to someone in peril.

Faith without WORKS - SOME ELBOW GREASE – is dead.

 # WORD: ENEMY

HEARD THIS IN MY SPIRIT WHILE DRIVING - Sometimes God will have you SLEEPING WITH THE ENEMY - sometimes literally right up in your own home and maybe in your own bed...people who would KILL YOU (PHYSICALLY; YOUR CHARACTER, YOUR SPIRIT) if the Lord allowed. As much as we want God to change THEM, sometimes it is allowed to TEACH US strategy and/or to develop a strength in us we would not have otherwise developed.

 # UN-HEALED MINISTERS

Omonpee has experienced a lot of people ministering NEGATIVELY out of REJECTION and BITTERNESS lately - on FB and otherwise. Speaking from experience (having been rejected), I encourage you to allow yourself to be HEALED and DELIVERED before you speak to or over God's People.

Hurting people hurt other people. And, DISCERNING people know that what you are saying is coming from a place of PAIN that is NOT BEING DEALT WITH PROPERLY; you will not be received and will cause you to FEEL even more REJECTED.

Break the cycle and be free!

 # HOW ARE YOU?

Asking people how they are doing ONLY BECAUSE you want them to ask you how you are doing so that you can tell them what you REALLY wanted to tell them in the first place (i.e., what you are going through) is a form of MANIPULATION.

Manipulation is, in the biblical sense, WITCHCRAFT.

Love, OWP

 ## VISION-LESS

I received another request for someone to "follow" me on Twitter. Only last week, I told someone that I don't know how to use it and have the account "by accident"☺. I was reflecting on how people are asking to FOLLOW me, but Twitter-wise, I'm not going anywhere :-). Then, the Lord showed me how people are FOLLOWING PASTORS who are not going anywhere because they have no vision.
WITHOUT A VISION, THE PEOPLE PERISH.

 ## WORD: DON'T QUIT

JUST HEARD THIS IN MY SPIRIT FOR SOMEONE WHILE REFLECTING ON MY OWN LIFE - When you are CALLED AND ANOINTED to MINISTER TO PEOPLE, to HELP PEOPLE, to SHARE WITH PEOPLE...you can rest and be assured that the enemy will cause you to be HURT by people, REJECTED by people, BETRAYED by people. This is to MAKE YOU LEERY of reaching out to people
and being TRANSPARENT.
Make up in your mind to strive toward PURPOSE and push past the hurts, disappointments, rejections and betrayals to do what He told you to do.

 ## STEWARDSHIP

With GREAT PURPOSE on our lives, we must be mindful of the ground into which we sow. Be led of the Lord in all things. Be careful of where you give your tithes and offerings and where you spend your money. Being a good steward is more than not spending frivolously; it is also WISE DISBURSEMENT.

 **"LET NOT..."**

Omonpee is meditating on "LET NOT your heart be troubled." "LET NOT" means that it is a CONSCIOUS DECISION and an ACTION on our part. When things happen, we can CHOOSE to LET our hearts be troubled or CHOOSE to NOT LET our hearts be troubled. We have both the choice and the power; it's up to us.

 *NO SWEATING*

"Never let 'em see you sweat."??? No...Just DON'T SWEAT! (Who cares what they SEE anyway? :-))
It CAN be done.
Move from a state of "ACTING LIKE" to "BEING."
"Acting like" is from without; "BEING" is from WITHIN.

"And he saith unto them, Are ye so without understanding also? Do ye not perceive, that whatsoever thing from without entereth into the man, [it] cannot defile him;

Because it entereth not into his heart, but into the belly, and goeth out into the draught, purging all meats?

And he said, That which cometh out of the man, that defileth the man." - Mark 7:18-20 KJV

 ## I CAN WALK!

"Yea, though I WALK....." I am stopping and praising Him right there - because I CAN WALK!! (Those who know, know why.) THANK YOU GOD!

 ## GREAT EXPECTATIONS

We flick on a light switch in EXPECTATION that the light will come on, no questions asked. When UPS or Fed Ex says they will deliver a package on a certain date, we EXPECT it then, no questions asked. Why then do we DOUBT and have LITTLE TO NO EXPECTATION when God promises or tells us He will do something for/in us? Our minds MUST be renewed in the area of faith.

 ## WORD: IDOLS

HEARD THIS IN MY SPIRIT FOR SOMEONE - Somebody said, "Lord, I'll serve in ministry when I get....(whatever it is; a spouse, a better job, more money, a house, deterrent of your choice)." But, God says, "Until you serve in ministry, you will not get...(whatever it is; a spouse, more money, a house, deterrent of your choice)."

You have already put it BEFORE GOD, therefore making it an IDOL. If you had "it" now, you still wouldn't serve God. He has to BE ABLE TO TRUST YOU TO DO RIGHT WITH IT before He can bless you.

PROFESSIONS

Singers sing. Teachers teach. Writers write. Preachers preach. Your PROFESSION is that that you PROFESS to be. And, PROFESSION without ACTION - i.e, FAITH without WORKS - is dead. If you are PROFESSING but have no intentions of ACTING, then, at some point, you are LYING.

PREACH AGAINST SIN

IF I LOSE FBFS BEHIND THIS, SEE YA, BUT... - I understand preaching the GOOD NEWS of the Gospel and not passing judgment, etc., but, doggone it, SOMEBODY'S GOTTA PREACH AGAINST SIN! Not necessarily against the PERSON but against the ACT! Even Jesus confronted the sellers in the temple with their WRONGDOINGS.

Do we expect people to KNOW THROUGH "OSMOSIS" that what they are doing is wrong, especially when it has become HABIT for them or when "Mama did it this way and Grandmamma before her did it this way"?

No, that stuff has to be broken!

The Ten Commandments themselves (which are CERTAINLY not the only commandments we have as Christians) are a list of "THOU SHALT NOTs". How in the world would you even PREACH or TEACH about those without talking about SIN/TRANSGRESSION? This new false doctrine that is going around that says that we ought not to mention SIN flies right in the face of the Ten Commandments. And, while those are in the OT and not in the NT, Jesus said that DID NOT COME TO DESTROY THE LAW, but to FULFILL it.

Love, OWP

WORD: TRUE RICHES

HEARD THIS IN MY SPIRIT AS I WALKED BACK
INTO THE HOUSE - "The BLESSING OF THE LORD
MAKETH RICH and HE ADDETH NO SORROW with
it." - Proverbs 10:22 KJV ...If it's causing you more
problems than it's worth and/or if it's causing you
more grief than it's worth, then it is not of the Lord.

EATING WITH ENEMIES

HE prepares a table before us in the presence of your
enemies, but it is up to us to EAT. Can you EAT in front
of people who are soooo hoping you would "choke"
and "die?" Or, are you AFRAID that you will "make a
mess" or "choke" and be laughed at by your enemy? Are
you sitting there STARVING with God's Provision right
in front of you, out of FEAR of what someone will say?
HE prepares the table, but it is up to us to eat.

SON-RISE

SUNRISE - During my prayer/meditation time this
morning, I thought about the phrase, "The sun is
rising." It is a MISNOMER. The truth is, the earth
ROTATES, but THE SUN DOES NOT MOVE UP AND
DOWN. When we -Earth- change, we cannot see it until
we rotate toward it again.
REVELATION - "Jesus Christ (THE SON) THE SAME,
YESTERDAY, and TODAY, and FOREVER." - Heb. 13:8
He never leaves US, but we sometimes
TURN AWAY FROM HIM.

IT TAKES ALL THAT

For people who tell you, "It (spirituality, ministry, marriage, something about which you are passionate) does not take all that!", it COULD BE that it does not take all that FOR THEM and/or they are too SCARED or LAZY to do it.

REVELATION: What God has spoken TO YOU, FOR YOU...PURSUE IT with fervor and don't let anyone talk you out of it!

ULTERIOR MOTIVES

When people offer to do things for you "out of the kindness of their heart", be sure that their heart really is KIND. Sometimes, in some people's minds, help = I-did-something-for-you-so-now-you-owe-me. Granted, God can use ANYONE to bless you, but use wisdom in whether the offer to help is from God or from a person with ulterior motives.

LAYING DOWN LIFE

Omonpee has been meditating on John 15:13-15, particularly as it relates to "laying down your life for a friend." People have taught this as Jesus speaking of crucifixion, but He was also (and, maybe REALLY) speaking of MINISTRY. When we are willing to deny our own desires, dreams and hopes in pursuit of living a life of selfless ministry to others, we have LAID DOWN OUR LIVES.
We have CRUCIFIED OUR FLESH.

Love, OWP

 ## STUMBLING

I had on a new, ill-fitting pair of sandals today at the museum...and TRIPPED OVER THE SIDEWALK :-)! I remember a time I would have stopped to see who SAW ME STUMBLE. But, I got an inbox earlier this week that changed me forever! In it, someone told me that, years ago, they saw me STUMBLE spiritually, but were blessed by my ability to RECOVER AND WALK ON! Today, my focus was not on STUMBLING, but WALKING ON! Glory!

 ## WORD: BEING IN HELL

HEARD THIS IN MY SPIRIT JUST NOW - Sometimes, God allows us to RESIDE IN HELL...so we can STRAIGHTEN HELL OUT (Luke 16:28 KJV; Rev. 1:18 KJV) and so we can KNOW within ourselves WE ARE CAPABLE of doing so.

Somebody has been in a HELLACIOUS situation for YEARS and it feels like a PRISON SENTENCE; an unrelenting NOOSE around your neck. You used to BEG and PLEASE with God to get out ("Please release me; let me go!") but you have now gotten to the point where you have GIVEN UP and have ALL BUT LOST HOPE.

God said that He would have you RELINQUISH YOUR OWN WILL TO HIM and allow Him to USE YOU to DO A WORK IN THE SITUATION. If YOU LEAVE THE SITUATION ON YOUR OWN WILL, you will see it again in another form and have to do your first works over. Allow Him to do the work in you and through you in THIS HELL so that you will not lose the time and effort you have already put in. Once you learn this, all other HELLS (and yes, there will be others) will seem minor.

 ## SWORD PLAY

What good is having a sword (or any other weapon) if we don't know how to use it? Or, if we are too out of shape and out of practice to wield it? The Word of God is our SWORD. But, if we do not STUDY CONSISTENTLY and MEDITATE ON IT DAY AND NIGHT...???

 ## WORD: OUR BABIES

HEARD THIS IN MY SPIRIT JUST NOW - Moses' mother, in an effort to save him, sent him down the Nile in a basket. God arranged for Pharaoh's daughter to find him and for Moses' mom to take care of him, with his sister Miriam watching for him throughout his entire journey in the basket.

REVELATION: Sometimes, when we have done all we can for our "babies", we

HAVE TO TURN THEM OVER TO GOD.

He can take care of them better than we ever could.

 ## "TWINKLE, TWINKLE..."

"Oh, minute celestial fixed luminous point! How I ponder your gaseous makeup, metaphysical characteristics and your ultimate role in the universe!"

TRANSLATION: "Twinkle, twinkle little star! How I wonder what you are!"

REVELATION: Do not get caught up in ministers using BIG WORDS and SOUNDING IMPORTANT. Hear with your SPIRITUAL EARS and DISCERN what is really being said.

GOSPEL OF PEACE

How ignorant is it to ARGUE AND FIGHT over A GOSPEL OF PEACE? Seriously!

PERKS & PROCESS

People who want what you perceive as the "PERKS" of my ANOINTING should also want the PROCESS I went through to flow in it. IF I make it look "EASY", it's because it NOW FLOWS out of me. The Word (water) flows out; the Anointing (oil) flows out. BUT...water and oil are SUPPOSED to FLOW OUT OF a BROKEN VESSEL! If you want the ANOINTING, then WANT THE PROCESS, too!
And, then, want it for the RIGHT REASON.

ORIGINS

JUST HEARD THIS IN MY SPIRIT FOR SOMEONE; DON'T THINK I WILL GET MANY AMENS :-) - With this many Mother's Day, many people are celebrating and reminiscing on happy times in the past. However, some people find it hard to so because they, for whatever reason, are ASHAMED of where they come from and/or of their past.

We must learn to EMBRACE our beginnings - however humble, painful, or unpleasant - and not be embarrassed of where we came from. First of all, we really had NO CHOICE in the matter; wherever we came from is where God CHOSE for us to come from, even before the foundation of the earth. Secondly, ALL

THINGS WORK TOGETHER for our good - even our ORIGINS.

I would not trade ANYTHING for my originS (plural). They truly made me who I am in God today.

GLORY VS. STORY

Omonpee got her hair done yesterday - relaxer, color (rinse; Lord showed me grape mixed with jet black; looks great!) and cut (in a bob, so that it is short in the back). My scalp was sensitive and I have a MAJOR perm burn EXPOSED in the back of my head. Yet, EVERYBODY keeps telling me how NICE my hair looks... as if they cannot SEE the burn.

REVELATION: People SEE your GLORY, but don't know your STORY :-).

DAILY BREAD

"Give us THIS DAY our DAILY BREAD." The Bread represents the Word of God; INSTRUCTIONS, SPIRITUAL SUSTENANCE. So, then, "give us this day our daily INSTRUCTIONS." Instructions are given FOR ASSIGNMENT and on a NEED-TO-KNOW basis. God does not brief me on your instructions, nor you on mine.

REVELATION - I thank God for being able to mind my own business and for not needing to know everything about everything and everything about everybody; too much responsibility. I also thank God that I do not know everything at once

73

FULL HARD DRIVE

Once, I had a (now older) PC. I let the HARD DRIVE get FULL...FULL of not just MY files, but OTHER PEOPLE'S files, files of PEOPLE/CLIENTS no longer in my life, useless FILES, frivolous files. Oh, yeah, and a couple of TROJAN HORSE viruses, too! My HARD DRIVE CRASHED and I had to pay GOOD MONEY to have it fixed and get another hard drive.

Once, I had a BRAIN/MIND and a SPIRIT that had gotten tired and weary. In addition to my OWN "issues", I had taken on ISSUES of people who were – for whatever reason – no longer in my life and/or who REFUSED to deal with their OWN ISSUES. I TOOK ON BURDENS and/or INTERNALIZED a lot of "foolishness" as a result. And, as a result, my SPIRITUAL HARD DRIVE CRASHED! God allowed me to go through PHYSICAL AILMENTS to cause me to RUN A DIAGNOSTIC on what I had DOWNLOADED and UPLOADED into my SPIRIT.

REVELATION – "Let a man EXAMINE himself..." We must run a spiritual DEFRAG every now and again and allow the Lord to SHOW US what is in us. Some things that we are going through are things that God has not ORDAINED that we go through; some are ALLOWED because we CHOSE to DOWNLOAD/UPLOAD some things into our SPIRIT and ended up with all manor of SPIRITUAL TROJAN VIRUSES - "These kind only come out by fasting and praying...

 ## FEELINGS

I am not moved by my "feelings." Day before yesterday, I "felt" happy and ready to take over the world. Yesterday, I felt "down." Today, I "feel" better than yesterday (praise the Lord). But, NO MATTER HOW I FEEL the Work of the Gospel has to be done. We cannot base what we do for Christ on our emotions; God is not moved by emotions and neither should we be.

 ## DRIED GLUE

If you are the GLUE that holds your FAMILY, BUSINESS OR MINISTRY together, if the GLUE DRIES OUT, things will fall apart.

REVELATION: WORKAHOLICS (such as myself), learn to GET SOME REST.
What good is the salt if it has lost its savor?
What good is the GLUE if it has lost its stickiness?

 ## GRACE HAS LIFTED

Omonpee has learned that when something she has done with ease and enthusiasm becomes cumbersome and a source of vexation, grace has probably lifted and it is time to leave it alone and move on. Grace is given for the assignment; when Grace lifts, the assignment is over...period.

 # SPRING FEVER

It seems that Spring Fever has hit the church, too! There seems to be an influx of posts regarding "giving up" and "heading for greener pastures" in terms of returning back to a life of sin. Be encouraged and hold on! Be INSTANT, in season and out of season! Remember, "April showers bring May flowers." (And, for the "deep" folk: "...weeping may endure for a night, but JOY cometh in the morning."- Psalms 30:5 b-c KJV)

 # CONTAINED THREAT

People talk about a "church without walls." I am just about of the opinion that with some of this stuff that goes on in "churches", we may need to CONTAIN it within the walls, until such time as it is dealt with. We don't need RELIGION, HYPOCRISY, SELF-RIGHTEOUSNESS, GOSSIPING, BACKBITING AND GREED gettin' out and FURTHER CONTAMINATING the poor unsaved people.
A QUARANTINE may be in order!

 # WORD: SHOWTIME

HEARD THIS IN MY SPIRIT FOR SOMEONE: Do not be moved by recession/depression. In a FAMINE, Joseph SHONE BRIGHTLY, after sitting in a dungeon for YEARS, falsely accused & forgotten. IT'S NOT TOO LATE! Go find YOUR COAT OF MANY COLORS, dust it off (or get it out of pawn) & put it on.
You are a STAR and He's been PREPARING YOU to PLAY THE ROLE YOU WERE BORN TO PLAY!
He's BRINGING YOU CENTER STAGE.
IT'S SHOWTIME, BABY!

STEP ON THE GAS

I was attempting to merge onto the interstate when a car in the right lane would not slow down or move over (it could do both) to let me in. I had to INCREASE MY SPEED, MATCH and EXCEED ITS SPEED in order to NOT MISS MY OPPORTUNITY TO MERGE. In doing so, I PASSED and SURPASSED the car, got in the right lane, and went on to my destination; once I passed the car, I did not see it again.

REVELATION: God said that sometimes HE ALLOWS people and situations to be put in your path who SEEM TO BE OBSTACLES. HE does this to make you COME ON UP! But for the haters, many people would NEVER PRESS IN AND PRAY; many would be content to keep going "the same road" and would not have a SENSE OF URGENCY about "finishing the course."

God uses these OBSTACLES to LIGHT A SPIRITUAL FIRE under us so that we will be PROVOKED to DO SOMETHING DIFFERENT. WE THINK that we are doing it to GET AWAY FROM THEM or to AVOID A "COLLISION" WITH THEM, but, really, God has ORCHESTRATED THIS RUN-IN to PROVOKE US to NOT BE COMPLACENT, but to "STEP ON THE GAS" and get on down the road to our PLACE OF DIVINE DESTINY.

Love, OWP

END OF THE WORLD

Omonpee is sooooo not moved by these so-called "end-of-the-world-on-May 21-rumors" nor the "end-of-the-world-in-2012-rumors." Truth is, it's the END OF THE WORLD for SOMEBODY EVERYDAY. Those of us who are busy doing Kingdom work HERE may "send up timber" but we are too busy to dwell on "up-pa yonder."

SAME OLD TRICKS

I wanted to be surprised at how people keep falling for these SAME OLD FB VIRUSES/HOAXES. One would think by now that people would KNOW NOT to CLICK ON STRANGE LINKS, that there is NO DISLIKE BUTTON and you CANNOT find out WHO HAS BEEN VIEWING YOUR PROFILE, especially since these hoaxes have cycled through so many times. But...then God REMINDED me of HOW OLD THE ENEMY'S TRICKS ARE and
HOW WE KEEP FALLING FOR THEM!(Ouch!)

RETURNING TO VOMIT

Once you have made a decision to STOP doing something that is sinful, harmful to you other others, that wastes your time and energy, and/or something that the Lord has just outright told you to STOP or LEAVE ALONE, do not let ANYONE make you TALK ABOUT IT, DWELL ON IT or RETURN TO IT AGAIN.

REVELATION - "As a dog returneth to his vomit, [so] a fool returneth to his folly (FOOLISHNESS)."
- Proverbs 26:11 KJV

 *CUSTOMS*

I was taught not to waste food growing up. Life has taught me not to waste money :-). So, I go to this Mexican food restaurant that has "all-you-can-eat"; the catch is that you CANNOT take anything out. I ONLY WANT THREE things on the plate (there are about 6 things and the servings are HUGE) and it is cheaper to buy the special than just the three things.

"Right" says, "Don't waste the food! Eat everything on your plate." But, GOD - RIGHT - has instructed me not to eat food just because it is there. It is not good for my health. So, what do I do (asking hypothetically)? Do I adhere to TRADITION AND SOCIETAL standards of "right"? Or, do I obey GOD'S COMMANDMENTS TO ME and do what He has told me to do?

We must weight TRADITION AND CUSTOMS against GOD'S WORD and HIS COMMANDMENTS TO US AND FOR US. While those traditions and customs served a purpose in times past, they may not line up with what He is saying to us for us. No matter what Mamma an' nem said or Granny Great said, it boils down to what HE SAID. His Right is Right!

REVELATION: "There is a way that SEEMETH RIGHT unto a man, but the end thereof ARE THE WAYS OF DEATH." - Proverbs 16:25 KJV

EATING THE EATER

I ♥ CRABLEGS (snow, dungeness and blue)! I have been eating them like crazy lately! I found it ironic that the scientific classification/name for CRABS is CANCER (hence, the zodiac sign)... Less than two years ago, CANCER was EATING ME UP and NOW I AM DEVOURING IT! :-)

WORD: OTHER "WIVES"

Just felt this in my spirit for someone: Male ministers, please be mindful of female parishoners/followers of your ministry who are so quick to "verbally" defend you against other people. Some of that is not "defending you" as much as it is "marking their territory." This is bad enough, but in most instance, the female in question IS NOT EVEN THE FIRST LADY/THE MINISTER'S WIFE!

If other females cannot comment on your status without JEZEBEL cutting in and wanting YOUR AFFIRMATION and ATTENTION, that is not "protecting you." That is something else. And, if you ALLOW it to happen, you like it and there is something you are getting out of it. If it makes you feel good to have a BUNCH OF WOMEN fighting over you and vying for your attention, then you are not running a ministry; you are RUNNING A HAREM and need to be delivered.

WORD: A NEW NAME

"I DIDN'T KNOW YOU BY YOUR NEW NAME!" - When some of my FBFs (female) married, their last names changed. When they sent me a Friend Invitation, I did not readily know who they were, especially if they did not have a picture posted. Some of them (like O.W.) started going by different FIRST NAMES, too; I DID NOT KNOW THEM BY THEIR NEW NAMES. REVELATION: When you give your life to God, He changes "your name." In the Bible, the name change was a literal one at times (Jacob to Israel; Saul to Paul; Abram to Abraham; Sarai to Sarah). Each of these name changes had SIGNIFICANCE because the NEW NAME had a MEANING that COINCIDED with GOD'S PURPOSE for that person's life.

I hear the Lord say that people who used to call you "THIEF" cannot find you under that name; now you are called "BLESSED." People who used to call you "HARLOT" now must call you "Virtuous Woman." Those who knew you as "REJECTED" will now come to know you as "BELOVED." Maybe you used to be known as "GREEDY" with a nickname of "STINGY"; people who knew you then can hardly believe that you go by "GENEROUS GIVER" now.

And, when the enemy comes to find you and calls you by your old name, HE CANNOT REACH YOU because YOUR CONTACT INFORMATION HAS CHANGED. Your NAME IS DIFFERENT and you DON'T EVEN LIVE IN THE SAME KINGDOM ANYMORE. "We're sorry, but you have reached a SOUL that has been DISCONNECTED from the KINGDOM OF DARKNESS..." GLORY!

KNOWING THE WORD

Gayle Garrett has become a dear real-life friend to me. We met on FB through Emily Webster, a dear real-life friend and confidante. Since that time, Gayle and her husband have read BOTH of my books REPEATEDLY (lost track of how many times). In both my and her times of "distress", Gayle has QUOTED BACK TO ME what "Prophetess Petcoff wrote in her books!"

It has ministered to me GREATLY that she knows my books better than I do :-) and that they help her (and me) SO MUCH!

REVELATION - When we STUDY GOD'S WORD, we become CLOSER TO HIM. "In the beginning was THE WORD, and THE WORD was WITH GOD and THE WORD...WAS...GOD." (John 1:1) THE WORD = GOD. When we spend time with THE WORD, we are spending time WITH GOD; we are becoming CLOSER TO HIM. It takes our relationship from one of just knowing that He exists to KNOWING HIM.

And, when we know HIS WORD, in times of peril and distress, we can QUOTE HIS WORD BACK TO HIM. Unlike Prophetess Petcoff :-), He does not FORGET what He has said (because Prophetess Petcoff writes under the anointing and when it lifts, she does not remember because it is not her saying it, but Him through her and she is merely a radio broadcasting HIS Transmissions ☺). But, when we quote His Word back to Him, we are ourselves REMEMBERING His Promises to US.

SPIRIT OF NOADIAH

THE SPIRIT OF NOADIAH : "My God, think thou upon Tobiah and Sanballat according to these their works, and on the prophetess Noadiah, and the rest of the prophets, that would have put me in fear."
– Nehemiah 6:14 KJV

REVELATION: If you, like Nehemiah, are "doing a great work so that [you] cannot come down", you can rest & be assured that there is a NOADIAH watching you to DISCOURAGE YOU and MAKE YOU AFRAID.

Noadiah was a female prophet/a PROPHETESS who had sided with and gave counsel to Tobiah and Sanballat, enemies of Nehemiah and his call to rebuild the wall. When Tobiah and Sanballat could not stop him, they joined forces with Noadiah. Noad...iah, who the scripture show to be a PROPHETESS, actually MISUSED her gift in an attempt to DISSUADE Nehemiah from doing what God said do.

God said that when you have dug in your heels and made up you mind that, come hell or high water, you are going to do what He said, the enemy knows that he cannot STOP you from going forward. He then sends those WHO LOOK LIKE YOU (as Nehemiah himself was a prophet) to get next to you and speak into your life words that will make you DOUBT who you are, what He said and if it will really work or not. These people come in the Name of the Lord and SEEM to have your best interest at heart. Do not be deterred by them, saith the Lord, but continue to PRESS FORWARD and "build the wall" that He has told you to build.

Love, OWP

WORD: DON'T HATE

JUST HEARD THIS IN MY SPIRIT - You cannot allow
the devil to continue to whisper in your ear and then
expect to HEAR PROFOUND REVELATION to give to
God's People. You cannot continue to PLAY FOOTSIE
with the devil (sometimes literally, too) and then expect
to WALK SURE-FOOTEDLY as a prophet
or any other type of minister.

And, you ought not HATE on those who CHOOSE to
LOVE THE LORD with their whole heart and can do
the EXPLOITS that you USED TO BE ABLE TO DO.

DIFFERENT STROKES

I tried to do what my friend did and drink this HOT,
HOT, HOT tea that she drinks everyday, all day. I LIKE
HOT TEA and thought I could handle it...but she likes
hers the temp of MOLTEN LAVA.
One sip and I burned my tongue :-).

REVELATION: "Now the world don't move to the beat
of just one drum. What might be right for you, may not
be right for some. It takes DIFFERENT STROKES to
move the world. Hmmmmm." LOL
(Theme from "Diff'rent Strokes)

(And that "HMMMMM" is me
holding my scorched tongue ☺. LOL)

84

HIDING IN THE OPEN

Watching "Undercover Boss." I usually forget that it's on and catch it from my FAVORITE PART: THE REVEAL!
I LOVE to see the employees' faces when they REALIZE who "Joe Schmo" really was/is.

REVELATION: God said that He has had you HIDDEN, right out in the open...maybe even from YOURSELF. But, at an APPOINTED TIME, He will REVEAL - to OTHERS AND TO YOU - WHO YOU REALLY ARE and THE AUTHORITY IN WHICH YOU WALK!

HEALTH SELF-ESTEEM

ON SELF ESTEEM - In Romans 12:3c-d, Paul admonishes them not to think MORE HIGHLY of themselves than they ought (he then talks about being sober-minded in this). "MORE HIGHLY" denotes EXCESSIVE. However, it does not say that we SHOULD NOT THINK HIGHLY of ourselves. God thinks highly of us and we are made in HIS IMAGE.

We must learn to see ourselves - good, bad, and ugly - as HE sees us and LOVE OURSELVES AND EACH OTHER according to HIS LOVE FOR US.

HE IS >

SPIRITUAL EQUATION:
He that is in me > He that is in the world

Love, OWP

BEDTIME POEM 2

REPOST: "Blessed Naptime" (Something silly I made up today, sung to the tune of "Blessed Quietness")

Joys are flowing
From my pillow
And my comforter is warm.
...Rain outside is
Falling softly.
Bye! A nap is coming on.

Blessed quietness,
Oh, the quietness!
Gone to curl up in a ball.
If you need me
While I'm sleeping
Use the inbox or my wall.

THE WHEEL

Omonpee is not a big fan of that song, "Jesus, Take the Wheel" (too sad and some people don't let Him have the wheel until they are about to wreck), but, doggone it, I have experienced it from the Jesus standpoint here of late. One minute this person wants me to take charge; the next, they are taking over.
Back and forth, give control away then take it back.
Poor Jesus! That's how we do HIM.

I LOVE MINISTERING!

standing up from the computer chair, looking out, somber voice

Hello, my name is Omonpee, and I am a MINISTRY-OHOLIC. I love ministering and cannot seem to stop, even when I should be sleeping. As quickly as I give out of what He gives me, He gives me new, fresh revelation to share; spiritually, it invigorates me. I love seeing people helped and I love helping, even if it is at the expense of my sleeping/resting ☹.

GO, GO, GO

"GO...ye, therefore..."
GET TO STEPPIN'!

MINISTER MINISTRY

THE PENDULUM SWINGS AGAIN -I noticed that I am back to ministering to MINISTERS in this season. I used to be used of God like this ALL THE TIME, but then then season changed and I ministered mostly to others. Interesting! I feel a very APOSTOLIC mantle on me right now.
IF I post something that you don't understand, the chances are probably pretty good that it's not intended for you (I'll try to specify as I remember ☺).

Love, OWP

⬱ RIGHT VS. CORRECT ⬱

There CAN BE a DIFFERENCE between BEING
CORRECT and BEING RIGHT, as it relates to BEING
RIGHT IN THE EYES OF GOD.
But, we cannot be RIGHT without CORRECTION.

⬱ ADDICTIONS ⬱

Many people who know me personally can attest to the
fact that, up until recently, I had a VORACIOUS
CAFFEINE ADDICTION (Pepsi and Coke). I KNEW it
was not good for me, but COULD NOT KICK THE
HABIT ON MY OWN. But, WHEN MY THYROID
WAS REMOVED, my body changed.

Now, while I WANT the caffeine, the CARMEL
COLOR messes with me; it makes me feel "icky." The
more I drink, the ickier I feel ;-). It gets to the point
where the "BENEFIT" of the caffeine is GROSSLY
OUTWEIGHED by SEVERITY of the ICKY FEELING.

REVELATION: Sometimes, the VERY THING,
PERSON, RELATIONSHIP that you feel that you
cannot live without is the very thing that you should
not have. When God has a GREAT CALLING on your
life and when you have SUBMITTED to Him, He "will
not leave you comfortless." And, no matter what it is,
"He will, with the temptation, make a way of ESCAPE."

I hear Him saying that there are some of you who are
UNCOMFORTABLE in relationships/situations/places

88

NOW that you were comfortable in only last year (last month). He said this is because HE is causing the UNCOMFORTABLE/ICKY feeling. You have prayed to HIM for HIM to change the situation; LET HIM WORK.

PROBLEM(S)

"Woe be unto you when all men shall speak well of you! For so did their fathers to the false prophets."
- Luke 6:36 KJV

REVELATION: If people have a PROBLEM with you, that is THEIR PROBLEM not yours. But, if NOBODY has a PROBLEM with you, then YOU'VE got a BIG PROBLEM. In fact, YOU probably ARE the PROBLEM!

CANCEROUS CRUTCHES

Last year when the cancerous cyst was on my thyroid, it had been there so long until it had pressed against my vocal cords on the left side and WEAKENED THEM. But, in it their weakened state, the cyst was also SUPPORTING them; it had become a CRUTCH for them of sorts.

REVELATION: God said there are some of you who have some CANCEROUS CRUTCHES in your life. Some of those people/traditions/mindsets/attitudes that you have LEANED ON for so long are actually HARMFUL to you. In this season, God will reveal WHO and WHAT should be ATTACHED to you and, if you allow it, will REMOVE the CANCEROUS CRUTCHES who SEEM to be a HELP, but who are SLOWLY BUT SURELY KILLING YOU SOFTLY.

Love, OWP

CAREFUL MINISTRY

I had a hairstylist who wore VERY LONG, curved acrylic nails. My hair was short and she used Marcel irons to curl the back. TO KEEP FROM BURNING ME, she would use the tips of her nails to "touch" the hot irons when completing a curl. She told me, "BEFORE I BURN YOU, I'D BURN MYSELF."

REVELATION - I have developed this SAME mentality for MINISTRY! I am EXTREMELY CAREFUL how I HANDLE ANYONE GOD HAS ENTRUSTED to my care.

LOOK/SEE

WOKE UP WITH THIS IN MY SPIRIT: Everybody who is LOOKING is not necessarily SEEING.
Upon His Ascension, Jesus asked the Disciples, "Why standing there GAZING up into heaven ?"(Acts1:11 b) They were STARING/LOOKING INTENSELY but, after all that time with Him and all that teaching, STILL NOT SEEING.

THOUGHT: Oh, say, can YOU SEE??

 # AUTO-IMMUNE

SPIRITUAL AUTO-IMMUNE DISEASES - An auto-immune disease in one in which the body's defenses ATTACK the BODY; in essence, the BODY ATTACKS ITSELF. It causes pain, immobility, lethargy, shutting down of vital organs and,
in worst-case scenarios, even death.

REVELATION: "A HOUSE DIVIDED AGAINST ITSELF CANNOT STAND." When the BODY OF CHRIST WAGES ATTACKS ITSELF - other parts and members - NO GOOD can come of it.

 # DOUBLE-MINDED

One day YOU WILL;
the next day YOU WON'T.

Last year you DID;
this year, YOU DON'T.

Today YOU "IS";
Tomorrow YOU "AIN'T".

This morning YOU COULD;
This evening YOU "CA(I)N'T.

" REVELATION: "A DOUBLE-MINDED man is UNSTABLE in ALL HIS WAYS." - James 1:8 KJV

Love, OWP

WORD: STILL HERE

FELT THIS IN MY SPIRIT FOR SOMEONE: I'm still here! What the enemy meant for evil.... What you thought would kill me, only made me stronger. Keep talkin': Run tell dat.

PATINA

PATINA - I'm watching "American Pickers" and they came across an airplane propeller that has a nice PATINA to it. I have seen people on "Antiques Road Show" that CLEAN the PATINA off, thinking the item SHOULD look a certain way, based on their "definition" of clean. They INADVERTENTLY RUIN the item and DECREASE THE VALUE.

As it turns out, the PATINA - the change in color/brown or green film brought on by age - INCREASED THE VALUE of the item. The EXPERTS have to tell them the bad news; they RUINED what could have been a VALUABLE ANTIQUE.

REVELATION; God is showing me that we as MINISTERS (not talking about anyone else right now :-) of the Gospel MUST SEE PEOPLE THROUGH THE EYES OF THE SPIRIT. We cannot try to MAKE THEM into what WE PERCEIVE THEY SHOULD BE or even what OUR IMAGE OF "CLEAN" IS. OUTSIDE OF THINGS/BEHAVIORS that are a CLEAR VIOLATION to the Scriptures, we have to have the Mind of Christ as to how we "rebuke" or "scold" people if they are not CONDUCTING THEMSELVES in a manner that we think they should.

God cannot be put into a BOX and we have to understand that just because something may not be done the way that we do it, it does not mean that it is not being done right! We cannot PRESUME to know EVERYTHING ABOUT EVERYBODY AND EVERY WAY THAT GOD WILL MOVE AND USE A PERSON. And, it is not our business to do so. To try to make people (other ministers in particular, but other Christians as well) CHANGE and CONFORM to our way of DOING AND SAYING THINGS - especially as it relates to ministry - IS A SPIRIT OF RELIGION AND IS NOT OF THE LORD.

If we are not careful, we can inadvertently "clean" the spiritual patina off - THE ANOINTING - and the minister nor the ministry will have the APPOINTED/ORDAINED EFFECT that God intended.

GROWN BABIES

Lord, please deliver O.W. Petcoff from SPIRITUALLY INCONTINENT people; GROWN BABIES. They can't "HOLD WATER"; you can't "DEPEND" on them to HOLD anything, either. They need to be "PAMPERed" constantly and "HUGGIEd" to make sure that everyone "LUVS" them. They are always in some "MESS", too. My diaper changing days are over! (God bless you TRUE PASTORS! I just don't know HOW y'all do it!

Love, OWP

⬤ TRUE IMPORTANCE ⬤

ON BEING "IMPORTANT" - At the moment that we can stop ACTING "important", God can move in our lives, entrust us with PURPOSE, endow us with STRENGTH, infuse us with HIS KNOWLEDGE and them MAKE US IMPORTANT because we will, at that point, be IMPACTING LIVES for the greater good. People who are truly "important" rarely STRESS THEIR OWN "IMPORTANCE", they are TOO BUSY DOING what they are IMPORTANT at doing.

⬤ A CORRECT READ ⬤

My dear FBF wrote a very touching post on my wall. Her AUTO CORRECT changed some of the words (e.g., changed PROPHETIC to PATHETIC). It did this because while it knew the WORD that is most often used that "sounds like" or "resembles" the WORD(s), IT WAS NOT AWARE OF HER TRUE INTENT; the CONTEXT of what she was saying.

REVELATION: Before we try to CORRECT/CHASTISE someone for their expression of who they are in God/how He uses them and/or speaks to them, we have to make sure that we are "READING" them in the proper "CONTEXT." We cannot try to make another... person's ministry/gift fit into our mold for it. My ministry (and me) has been rejected so much and misunderstood even more. It used to really bug me, but I have come to understand that God allowed this (and, maybe even ordained this) for my making. It has caused me to open my spiritual eyes and spiritual ears to be able to see God being "presented" in unusual ways and by "unusual" people. I am thankful for this.

CUT 'EM OFF!

I am steeping tea in a pot on the stove, mistakenly using the teacup-sized bags. The paper tags on the ends kept falling into the steeping tea; I kept BURNING MY FINGERS trying to dig the little NUISANCES out :-). Finally, I got the idea to get the kitchen shears and SNIP them off. My fingers thank me:-).

REVELATION- If you keep getting BURNED in a situation/relationship, it may be time to "wake up and smell the TEA" and CUT SOME FOLKS OFF!

ABASE & ABOUND

Omonpee knows how to abase and abound.

I have driven and I have walked. I have salon-ed and I have "baseball-capped." I have dined in five-star restaurants and I have scraped up money for the value menu. I have been highly sought after and I have been picked last. I have had an "entourage" and I have been left alone to die.

Through it all, God has watched over me; He has kept me. That's why position, title and accolades do not faze me. Whether I'm high on the horse or lower than an ant's belly button, God is God and He's with me.

Love, OWP

 ## MATURITY

When Desmond was small, when I took him to the barber, I would almost need to come armed with a TRANQUILIZER DART GUN; he would squirm, jump and holler. TODAY, I took him and he sat there so MATURELY....
and EVEN GOT HIS MUSTACHE TRIMMED!
REVELATION: "When I was a child, I understood as a child, I spake as a child: but when I BECAME A MAN I PUT AWAY CHILDISH THINGS.' – I Cor. 13:11 KJV

 ## PULL OF REJECTION

When you have suffered rejection, it seems your mind is a compass that keeps pointing/steering you in the direction of those who reject you; you keep wanting to get their attention/approval if for no other reason to know WHY they are rejecting you. Purpose to BREAK FREE of the pull of rejection; the people who do not desire you are undeserving of your time and energy. Focus on those who embrace, accept and love you.

 ## USURPERS

USURPERS - In this season, be mindful of people who would attach themselves to you for the sole purpose of taking over the vision/ministry/work that you have prepared for all of your life and the labor for which you are beginning to enjoy the fruits. Share as God leads, but some will try TO TAKE IT ALL. For them, be as the Little Red Hen - "You didn't help me bake my bread and you won't help me eat it."

 # *MIDAS TOUCH*

Years ago, this prophet prophesied to me, saying "...and EVERYTHING YOUR HANDS TOUCH WILL TURN TO GOLD." People may not realize it, but this concept comes from Greek mythology and the story of King Midas. He "prayed" to the gods for this very gift. However, a curse came with it: He touched his daughter and she TURNED INTO SOLID GOLD.

REVELATION: Anointing comes with hardships, pain, sacrifice, suffering and "going through." To whom much is given, much is required. Be careful what you pray for and be wise enough to know it when you see it, embracing the path and pitfalls that it took to get to it. The pain is as much of the blessing as the payoff.

 ## MRS. HARPER

PEARLS OF WISDOM FROM MRS. HARPER (on the phone tonight)

MRS. HARPER: So Honey, tell me about what you've got going on next week (medical procedures for each day of the week next week).

ME: (I told her, with shots and labs, etc. two or three days in a row.)

MRS. HARPER: "Honey, I got so sick of the doctors when I was in the hospital.
They came in in groves, each with their hands out for some of my money. One of 'em drew blood all the time.
Every time I saw him coming,
I yelled, "HEY, DRACULA! "

ME: SCREAMING ROFL!

◉◉◉◉◉◉◉◉◉◉◉◉◉

Prophetess O.W. Petcoff

Author O.W. Petcoff is the wife of Ronald Petcoff and mother of Monisa Caldwell and Desmond Petcoff. Petcoff is the founder of ONOMA Ministries and Publications. She is also an ordained minister and Christian book writer. Prophetess Petcoff has ministered both nationally and abroad. She currently resides in Arlington, Texas.

◉◉◉◉◉◉◉◉◉◉◉◉◉